D1576112

WORLDS OF THE MENTALLY ILL

How Deinstitutionalization Works in the City

Dan A. Lewis, Stephanie Riger,
Helen Rosenberg, Hendrik Wagenaar,
Arthur J. Lurigio, Susan Reed

Southern Illinois University Press

Carbondale and Edwardsville

Library of Congress Cataloging-in-Publication Data

Worlds of the mentally ill : how deinstitutionalization works in the
    city / by Dan A. Lewis . . . [et al.].
      p.   cm.
      Bibliography: p.
      Includes index.
      1. Mentally ill—Deinstitutionalization.   I. Lewis, Dan A.
    RC439.5.W67   1991
    362.2—dc20   89-10056
    ISBN 0-8093-1477-0   CIP

FOR DOROTHY MILLER

CONTENTS

TABLES

ACKNOWLEDGMENTS

We gratefully acknowledge the support of the Chicago Community Trust and the Illinois Department of Mental Health and Developmental Disabilities. The grant we received from these two organizations made the research we are reporting here possible. We also appreciate the assistance we received from the Chicago Police Department and mental health professionals working at the four Chicago-area state hospitals where much of the data were collected.

As usual, the Center for Urban Affairs and Policy Research at Northwestern University proved to be a very supportive environment in which to do the research and writing. We wish to thank Janet S. Soule and Audrey Chambers for their help in preparing the manuscript.

The points of view expressed in this work do not represent the positions of either the Chicago Community Trust or the Illinois Department of Mental Health and Developmental Disabilities.

Finally, we wish to thank the hundreds of state mental patients who spent their time talking with us. We hope what we have written here reflects their experiences and leads to a mental health service system that is more responsive to their needs.

WORLDS OF THE MENTALLY ILL

1 INTRODUCTION

The present mental health system is generally recognized as unsatisfactory, but there is no consensus on how to improve it. Advocates of reforming the existing system would either augment community services or else place more patients in mental health institutions and increase the time they spend there. Those who feel that the system is beyond reform suggest that the only possible strategy is to adopt a policy of defensive management, meeting short-term objectives and dealing only with acute problems.

Much of the predicament arises from the persistence of outmoded concepts for describing and evaluating the social problem created by mental illness. These old notions, shared by the mainstream medical and social science communities, hide more than they reveal about the current mental health system and the people treated within it. Progress toward a better system requires clearer, more realistic thinking about this problem.

Defining the problem of mental illness in our society is no easy matter. After all what makes mental illness a problem? Is it the lack of resources we allocate to services? The lack of knowledge we have about its causes and prevention? The number of mentally ill in our society? How we define the problem will determine much of the later discussion about how we solve it. Gusfield (1975) has made the useful distinction between the container we use to hold a problem and the material that is contained. Both constitute what a social problem is. We use many containers to hold the problem of mental illness, and most distort the experience of those who are mentally ill and those who care for them. We will look at some of the containers currently used to hold the problem of mental illness and describe the distortion that has occurred. We will then provide our own container for the problem of mental illness and discuss how it provides for the integrity of the experiences of the mentally ill in our deinstitutionalized system of care.

The purpose of this book then is to develop a better container for describing and evaluating the mental health system and propose new directions in the care and control of the mentally ill. We first outline the limitations of the old concepts used to discuss mental illness and explain why they are no longer useful. We also develop a new set of analytic tools to assess the realities of the current system and suggest ways to improve it.

It is obvious to those who study the mentally ill that the mental health system has been radically transformed over the last thirty years. The mentally ill once were housed in large institutions far removed from civil society; now they are treated in a variety of settings, including but not limited to the state hospitals. Patients once spent long periods of time in segregated settings with few of the legal protections afforded to other citizens; now they make use of a variety of interrelated treatment settings in which they are afforded the same legal protections as any citizen.

The ideas and terms used to describe this new service policy have not kept pace with the changes. While the patient and mental health system have been deinstitutionalized, theories used to understand this new situation have not. We are still using ideas about the patient, his or her illness, and therapeutic settings that were formulated during the period in which institutions dominated mental health care. Consequently, we look in the wrong places to solve problems that concern us. Ideas that were sensitive to segregative practices and their effects on the mentally ill do not capture the realities of integrative, or, better, *inclusionary* systems and how they shape the lives of the mentally ill (Cohen, 1985). Cohen suggests that there are two contrasting modes of control, inclusion and exclusion, and that we can rewrite the history of social control as a choice between these two poles. Exclusion means banishment and segregation, while inclusion means assimilation and incorporation. We will use the term inclusion to capture the essential nature of the current mental health system. The consequence of this reliance on ideas that were meant to describe institutional care is that we overlook the impact of this new system on the patient and his or her care. Furthermore, what we cannot see and discuss, we cannot improve, so our lack of new containers affects our policy formulation.

This report focuses on the public mental health system in Chicago, the new system of care we have created, and its effect on the people served. More important, it deals with the inability of traditional conceptual tools to understand and describe today's system of mental health care and the experiences and needs of those served within it. We hope this book will lead to improvements in the Chicago system. At a minimum, we hope it will change the terms of the debate.

The Dehomogenization of the Mentally Ill

When the mentally ill were treated in large state institutions, both psychiatric and sociological theories viewed patients as if they were a homogeneous group. While it was a matter of great debate whether that homogeneity was caused by an illness or by a labeling process, there was an unspoken consensus that people who were severely mentally ill were alike in many important aspects.

Regardless of disease or label, patients were seen as victims. If their situation was to be made better, the system of care had to be changed. Because they were victims, the key to improvement lay in changing what others did to them. Because the state hospital was the central institution that cared for the mentally ill, it was the state hospital that would have to be transformed. Psychiatrists supporting the medical model fought bitterly with social scientists who used labeling theory. Both saw mental patients as *passive,* impelled by forces they could not control and sharing the characteristics (especially their behavior or symptoms) that made them different from the rest of society. Lost in this homogenization process were the factors other than disease and labels that affect how people behave. Inside large state institutions, these other factors are of little consequence for treatment or control, but once patients move outside, they become quite important.

By continuing to see the mentally ill as a homogeneous group after deinstitutionalization has removed the structures that create the illusion of similarity, we rely on a view of mental illness that does not do justice to the experience of the mentally ill in contemporary society. Race and gender, in particular, demarcate subgroups of patients whose experience with the mental health system is quite disparate. Black males, for example, have a history and pattern of community experiences quite different from that of black females, as we show in chapter 3. Retaining the image of patients as a homogeneous group seriously distorts our ability to see the problems of the mentally ill today.

There are three ways in which homogenization affects thinking about mental health policy. The first, discussed above, is that the mentally ill are thought of as uniformly passive, so that the existence of distinct subgroups within that category is not perceived, to say nothing of the different needs of these subgroups. The patient, whether a victim of an illness or of a labeling process, bears no responsibility for his or her problems and most importantly, it is the treatment system that must be changed if the patient is to be improved. The problem is not the person and how he or she behaves, but rather the system and how it treats the person. Change the system and you can fix the person. For the labeling theorists, the problem always lies in the treatment system, which must be dismantled; for the psychiatrists, it lies in expanding conventional treatment. Thus, homogenization shifts our attention from the mentally ill to those who treat them.

The debate becomes more complex as various professional groups compete to prescribe how the system is to be changed. Within the current context, this competition leads to divergent programs and clinical regimens over which the interest groups contest. This competition—called *guild innovationism*—is essentially a debate over which clinical program should be adopted. The mental health professions disagree over which programs ought to be introduced into the system of care, and the obvious turf fights over authority lie just below the surface of the public discourse.

The Societal Context of Mental Health Policy

Since the mentally ill are seen as a homogeneous group of victims, the key factors for policy makers have been their common illness and/or the process through which they are labeled ill. We call this tendency—to reduce the mentally ill to their illness—*mental health exceptionalism*. This leads to a very narrow focus in policy discussions on how the mentally ill, and this group alone, has fared over time and space. All that matters in the discussions is how to improve care for the mentally ill as a segregated group; little attention is paid to the experiences of other stigmatized and segregated groups such as the physically disabled, the criminal, or the mentally retarded.

This exclusive focus on the mentally ill and disregard for more general shifts in styles of social control or experiences of other disabled or deviant groups is evident in current policy discussions. The story of the problems of the mentally ill over the last twenty years is usually told as part of the history of the treatment of the mentally ill. The reforms that occurred in the 1950s and 1960s are seen as the latest chapter in the progress of therapeutic care and are thought to follow from professional judgments on how to treat the mentally ill. It is believed that humanitarian and professional concern led to innovations in treatment and that the factors that explain the innovations can be found in how reformers and professionals improve treatment. Yet, in fact, shifts in mental health policy have paralleled shifts in attitudes toward and services to other disabled or deviant groups. Deinstitutionalization of the mentally ill occurred at the same time as "mainstreaming" mentally retarded children and community corrections for delinquents, for example.

Mental health exceptionalism is the assumption that changes in mental health policy are based solely on our reactions to mental illness and our efforts to improve its treatment. This assumption leads to taking the pronouncements of mental health professionals and reformers (both medical and social scientists) at face value and looking only at these pronouncements and the history of mental health treatment for the antecedents of current policy. Patterns of reform that apply to other disabling statuses are not discussed, and reforms that affect larger groups in our society (e.g., minorities) are not seen as relevant to explaining the changes in mental health policy. When analysts of deinstitutionalization look only to previous mental health policies to explain changes, they ignore the possibility that what is happening to the mentally ill is part of a more general transformation at the societal level. Mental health exceptionalism limits the discussion to a narrow set of factors that may have little to do with actual causes of the changes in mental health policy. By ignoring patterns of change shared by the entire society, this exceptionalism treats the problems of the mentally ill as following from their disability, when they may be a consequence of factors affecting the entire society.

The Diminishing Power of the Mental Health Professional

We have left the debate about mental health policy to the professions that compete for control of care. Because the persons served by state mental hospitals are seen as homogeneous by virtue of their shared illnesses and situation, proposals for helping them usually involve the training of mental health professionals or the funding of innovative programs they design. For instance, Roesch and Golding (1985) analyzed the impact of deinstitutionalization and concluded that this strategy has not resulted in adequate care for patients. In order to address its shortcomings, they call for "appropriate adequate funds for community services, mental health professionals needed to provide more creative treatments instead of relying heavily on medication, and researchers needed to evaluate various treatment alternatives." For these authors, the problems of the mentally ill are primarily a function of mental disease and can be solved only by innovative efforts on the part of mental health professionals.

Unfortunately, it is this guild innovationism that created some of the problems faced by the contemporary mental health system, and it is unlikely that more of the same will improve matters. This is not to suggest that new therapeutic programs may not be worthwhile for some, but only that clinical innovations that involve client and professional are only a small part of the patient's life. Time in treatment is short, and the turnover among both professionals and clients in most clinical settings suggests that clinical interventions can have limited effects. By looking only to clinical innovation, the debate over improving policy is reduced to the promotion of favorite programs by different professional factions. Professionals promote programs that benefit their ranks and end up looking like special interests seeking their own welfare in the name of helping the mentally ill.

Reliance upon mental health professionals to solve the problems of the mentally ill is a strategy that made sense when the mentally ill were a passive group, isolated socially and economically from the center of society. As active participants in their communities, however, mentally ill people make choices that may or may not involve psychiatric treatment. When the residents of mental hospitals became citizens again, they regained some control over their treatment and the mental health professional lost some authority and control over their treatment. Many critics of mental health policy argue that the psychiatric professionals should be restored to the position of authority they held when patients and professionals were locked away from civil society. Furthermore, integration into civil society brought a whole set of problems for the mentally ill. Even if patients do choose to participate in a treatment program that focuses on their mental illness, the low economic status of many of them affects their utilization of services. However, many mental health professionals resist treating the panoply of problems that are not strictly mental. Bassuk and Gerson (1978) epitomize this perspective when they decry the nonpsychiatric nature of work within community mental health centers.

> Moreover, the centers' deviation from traditional methods of psychotherapy and their frequent preoccupation with nonclinical issues involving public health, social problems and economics have made many academic professionals reluctant to become engaged in community mental health programs. It is important that specific roles and tasks be defined for the personnel staffing the centers and that adequate recruitment and training programs be developed. (p. 52)

The fact is that therapy plays a relatively small role in the mental health delivery system as it is currently organized. Service workers within the Department of Welfare, Social Security, Medicaid, halfway houses, and shelters for the homeless interact regularly in order to maintain the mentally ill within the community. To focus exclusively upon the contribution that mental health professionals can make to the diverse problems of the mentally ill is to view their current situation with professional blinders.

The problems of the mentally ill have been defined in the following way: deinstitutionalization released the mentally ill from hospitals, so that they can no longer get the kind of treatment they need for their illness. The solution is to fund programs that will provide treatment outside the hospital. Yet the current mental health system involves much more than the release of patients from hospitals. As we will show, services for the mentally ill have become integrated into the service network of the poor. The state hospital has opened its doors to a variety of nonpsychiatric professionals, who exert as much influence on the lives of the mentally ill as do the psychiatric professionals who once ruled the roost. The policy of deinstitutionalization is often blamed for the inability of mental health professionals to treat the mentally ill. In fact, the transformation of the state hospital and its role in the service network has changed the position of the psychiatric professional in the lives of the mentally ill. The involvement of these professionals in every aspect of the patient's life—economic and social, as well as psychiatric—cannot be understood merely as "preoccupation with nonclinical issues."

Deinstitutionalization of Research on the Mentally Ill

What then is to be done? If guild innovationism, mental health exceptionalism, and the assumption of homogeneity of the mentally ill simply perpetuate the traditional system, how can we make progress? We must begin by understanding how the new system affects the lives of the mentally ill. We must shed the blinders just discussed and look as objectively as we can at the interaction between patients and services. We must take time to study the lives of state mental patients as they intersect our new inclusionary system. We must examine such key factors as how patients think about their illness and how treatment affects their relations with the service system. We must look at how race, gender, and income shape what patients do over time. Finally, and most importantly, we must dehomogenize the mentally ill and recognize the heterogeneity of people and the complexity of their lives in order to understand how this new system operates.

This book attempts to reach these goals by presenting findings from a long- term study of state mental hospital patients. We selected a random sample of patients and interviewed them three times to observe how they cope over time and how that coping is related to treatment in the mental health system.

The mentally ill person, especially in this era of deinstitutionalization, has to be viewed *in context*. Since state hospitals are only a part of the patient's context, we must illuminate how other settings (family, economic, and social) influence behavior. In other words, we must deinstitutionalize our research as we have deinstitutionalized the patients. This means not only looking outside institutions to understand the mentally ill but also studying the problems prospectively rather than retrospectively. Most institutional studies of mental illness work "backwards," that is, they relate factors about the patient's current status (admission, diagnosis, etc.) to previously documented aspects of the person (admissions, diagnosis, demographics, time in treatment, etc.) What we know about the mentally ill and government programs has been learned from this kind of work.

This approach reveals something about the background of those admitted to a hospital at some past time, but it cannot describe those who once were treated and did not return to the hospital. We will see in chapter 4 that working prospectively, tracking a group of patients and identifying their progress, transforms one's understanding of how patients cope.

A deinstitutionalized methodology has another important attribute. It brings to life the complexity and purposefulness of the patient's activities. Typical research designs reduce explanations of patient behavior to either disease or labels. These passive deterministic approaches have not shed much light on patients' behavior in the deinstitutionalized system. In their stead, we need approaches to studying mental illness that allow us to see how patients, their families, and professionals interact with, care for, and control the mentally ill. We need approaches that highlight the choices these patients make in the context of their lives. Family, income, job, and housing opportunities all set the stage for action by these people as they cope with mental illness. Mental health services are no longer the sole solution for the problems in living that the mentally ill have and create. Most patients must still find food, clothing, shelter, and comfort when the treatment is over and their chronic illness remains.

In our deinstitutionalized methodology a stratified sample of state mental patients was interviewed in three sequential waves. The first interview was conducted when the patients were residing in Chicago-area state hospitals, and the next two interviews, six and twelve months later, in whatever settings the patients were located. We administered questionnaires that focused on the patients' treatment, social networks, living situations, definitions of their mental illness, functioning level, diagnosis, and experiences with mental health services. Key measures were repeated at each interview so as to monitor constancy and change within the sample over time.

This effort was supplemented with a deeper, qualitative look at those within the sample who were readmitted to the state hospital during the course of the study. Interviews of a subgroup of readmitted patients, their families, and clinicians provided data that described how patients thought and behaved within their contexts. By doing our work prospectively we were able to study not only where patients had been but also how they lived in the community.

This report begins with a discussion of how state hospitals have changed over the last twenty years and the impact of this transformation on the rest of the system. Next, it presents a close look at the kinds of people who are treated in the state system. It then describes how patients who return to state hospitals experience readmission and how the troubles these patients experience outside the hospital lead to their rehospitalizations. We show that patients need income and intimacy to build lives for themselves in civil society and that both are in short supply among state mental hospital patients. We then discuss the consequences of the contemporary system for key issues of how patients function in the community, what kinds of criminal threat they pose to others, and what effect aftercare has on their ability to stay out of the hospital and do well in the community.

Finally, we review our findings and discuss implications of our study for the future of mental health services in urban areas. We discuss how community care has come to mean the privatization of mental health services and the commodification of patients. While privatization in itself is neither good nor bad, it has not delivered, at least in the mental health field, the results that were anticipated. The private sector has been ineffective in the care of state mental patients, and we suggest that more privatization is not likely to improve the situation, since the building blocks of a more successful life are not provided by the service industry. Indeed, if the experience of other human services can be a guide, privatization can lead to even less accountability by the state for the services it offers. We propose that the state deinstitutionalize its own services and offer the kinds of help (medication compliance, housing, and family support) that keep people in the community and to do it in ways that make the government accountable.

Every revolution in the care of the mentally ill has been defined by the new relationships created between patients and those who care for them (Havens, 1987). This was true of the creation of state hospitals and the introduction of Freudian analysis into the United States. The current system also transforms how patients relate to those who would help them. We are just beginning to understand these new relationships and how to improve them. We hope this study contributes to both that understanding and improvement.

2

THE STATE HOSPITAL AFTER DEINSTITUTIONALIZATION:

THE CONTEXT FOR CARE

On any given day at a state mental hospital in the Chicago area about two-thirds of its patients have been there (or to a comparable hospital) before. Almost no one stays for more than a month; most are released within two weeks. The patients are assigned to wards on the basis of their home address, so that patients from the same neighborhoods are housed on the same ward, regardless of diagnosis and functioning level. Assignments are made in this way so that release planning and aftercare placement are made easier. These facts represent profound differences between the way the hospital is operated today and the way it was operated twenty years ago. The context of care has been transformed, and that operation of the state hospital is at the center of the process.

If we are to make sense of the behavior of state mental patients in the city, we must first come to terms with deinstitutionalization, not as a slogan, but as a set of organizational arrangements that begin with the state hospital and how it operates.

In this chapter, we explore the changes in state hospitals over the last twenty years and suggest how those changes require a new approach to mental health policy. We challenge the conventional wisdom that the most important change in the operations of state mental hospitals was the release of many patients, what most refer to as *deinstitutionalization*. The mental health system has undergone an organizational transformation from a simple custodial institution to a web of public and private facilities. The contemporary state hospital is remarkable for the degree to which it is integrated into society, connected to the other institutions that sustain and control the mentally ill. That integration is least understood by those who lament the current state of mental health policy, but it must be understood if we are to improve the current ways we care for the mentally ill. It is more important to understand who has been let in to state hospitals than who has been let out.

The policy of deinstitutionalization began to be implemented **11** across the country during the 1970s. The state mental hospital has been changed by the influx of nonpsychiatric interests and professionals in the decision-making process, by the changed legal relationship between patients and therapists, and by a trend toward privatization of service delivery. Together, these forces reshaped the mental health system from one in which the mentally ill were segregated from the surrounding community to one in which segregation occurs for a very short period of time and the majority of patients' lives and concerns are centered *outside* the state mental hospital.

These changes cannot be understood simply as the misguided implementation of a policy of deinstitutionalization. While the policy shift that reduced the resident population of our state mental hospitals is significant, it cannot, by itself, explain the dynamic of the contemporary mental health system nor the role that the state mental hospital currently performs within the service system. Instead, a much broader analysis of the transformation is needed to place the reductions in residency rates within political and ideological contexts. Not only have patients been released from mental institutions after much shorter hospitalizations, but the authority structure within the institution has changed dramatically. Not only has civil rights legislation restricted the freedom of the hospital staff to commit the mentally ill, but the inclusion of legal aid attorneys in the ongoing processes of the state hospital has altered the relationship between professionals and clients. Moreover, not only are mental patients released from the hospital after much shorter stays, but they are referred to a network of services that they may or may not successfully navigate. Similar transformations have occurred in other institutions of social control, such as the prison and juvenile correctional system. Deinstitutionalization is more a consequence than a cause of two decades of change.

From this viewpoint, the current problems of the state mental health system look quite different. The debate within the mental health literature regarding the admission practices of the state mental hospital, which centers on the question "Is deinstitutionalization humane?" does not take into account the radical transformation that has occurred in that institution and in its role in the lives of the mentally ill. Similar changes that have occurred in other systems of social control are evidence that a historic paradigm shift has reshaped social service institutions. The policy of short-term hospitalization for the mentally ill must be viewed in the context of the larger process of which it is a part.

In fact, the contemporary state mental hospital plays such a different role in the lives of mental patients that its admission policies should not be the focus of the policy debate. Patients' economic status now determines how well they adapt to their new-found freedom. The current policy debate must consider the choices the mentally ill have to make in their use of services and confront the dependency to which even the sanest members of the underclass have been driven.

The Deinstitutionalization of Social Control

The discussion of deinstitutionalization has involved, in part, the debate over which historical forces have contributed to the policy shift away from custodial care. Various authors have argued the significance of one or another trend. Scull (1977) argued that fiscal pressure upon the state caused the cutback of funding to state institutions. Rothman (1980) emphasized the ideological shift of reformers away from reliance on the asylum routine toward a case-by-case approach in the treatment of deviance. Lerman (1982) pointed out that the trend toward deinstitutionalization actually coincides more closely with changes in income maintenance legislation, in which the federal government took over the funding of permanently disabled individuals through Supplementary Security Income (SSI). Others have equated deinstitutionalization with court rulings of the late 1960s and early 1970s that extended civil rights to inmates of state institutions, such as prisons and mental hospitals (Stone, 1982).

The purpose of this chapter is to demonstrate that modern changes in state funding, court rulings, and professional ideology have profoundly affected all institutions of social control, not simply mental hospitals. The shift away from custodial care in the mental health field has been paralleled in adult and juvenile correctional systems. While the adult correctional system has been affected by the trend toward community services, the traditional institution, the penitentiary, remains intact. The organization of the prison, once a highly segregated and insulated institution, has been profoundly altered, however. Jacobs (1977), when he described recent developments in the organization of the prison, argued that the administrative style of the penitentiary has been transformed by the extension of civil rights to prisoners.

In the 1970s, court rulings imposed upon prison administrators certain legal procedures by which the treatment of inmates would be subject to review. In addition, the penitentiary, which had been characterized by an insulated authoritarian structure, came increasingly under the scrutiny of the media and federal agencies as well as the courts. Jacobs argued that the imposition of legal standards and norms altered the style of administration in the prison, giving way to a more rational, bureaucratic form of management according to centrally established regulations and procedures. At the same time, the relationships between administrators, guards, and inmates were changed by the extension of citizenship rights to prisoners, establishing at least the formal prerogative to file a grievance. Also, unionization provided guards with leverage in their negotiations with administrators. In general, the administrators of the prison are now forced to interact with interest groups that seek to redress grievances or protect rights they see in jeopardy. The courts, media, enlightened administrators, unions, and groups purporting to represent the disenfranchised challenge how the institutions operate and promote reforms in attempts to extend rights or rectify wrongs.

This general process, which swept through many institutions after World War II, engulfed the state mental hospitals also. The patient was no longer seen as someone outside the protection of American citizenship. Rather, through the courts and other reform institutions, he or she was brought under the protection of rules and norms that rationalized his care and no longer allowed arbitrary treatment outside the rule of law. The extension of the social franchise to the mentally ill meant that others outside the hospital were concerned about treatment and would not leave the management of the institution to the dictates of its superintendent. This process had somewhat different effects on the state mental hospital and on the state penitentiary, an institution that did not move as far toward the privatization or deinstitutionalization of its social control function. In that way, the mental health system bears a closer resemblance to the system of juvenile corrections.

Lerman (1982) analyzed the effect of deinstitutionalization on the utilization of both youth and mental health facilities. He argued that research focusing on residency rate reduction in traditional state mental hospitals and juvenile correction centers does not take into account the dramatic changes that have occurred in both systems. For instance, the Juvenile Justice and Delinquency Prevention Act of 1974 (amended 1977) held that delinquent youth were not to be confined with adults; status offenders (juveniles who have not violated a criminal statute) and dependent and neglected children were not to be placed in juvenile detention or correctional facilities. Lerman demonstrated that while the traditional juvenile correctional institutions displayed the appropriate rate reductions in response to this policy shift, more young people than ever before were brought into the "nontraditional institutions" of the deinstitutionalized juvenile correctional system in a process that has been called "net-widening." For instance, nondelinquent youth are significantly less likely to be institutionalized in juvenile correctional facilities but more likely to be subject to "voluntary" admission to one of the growing number of facilities for "emotionally disturbed" youth in the mental health system. In addition, public funds were shifted to private entrepreneurs for the care of youth in trouble, the aged, and the mentally ill. Yet many of these private facilities do not achieve the standards set for public institutions by the new law.

The state mental health system has been affected by the same processes that have reshaped the penitentiary and the juvenile correctional system. The state mental hospital has adapted to legal reform and to pressures that it include a variety of interested parties, such as unions, in its organization. In addition, the institution now stands at the center of a network of public and private agencies that have taken over many of its functions. The beginning of this change is difficult to pinpoint, but we will begin the story in the mid-1940s.

The Transformation of the State Mental Hospital

Legislation that instigated reform of the mental health system in its present direction began toward the end of World War II. The size and isolation of state hospitals were to be changed by establishing many small community mental health clinics. The National Mental Health Act of 1946 provided training grants for mental health manpower, created networks of community clinics, and stimulated research into causes, diagnoses, and treatments of mental diseases (Donnelly, 1978; Ragan, 1974). The use of federal funds for the development of psychotropic drugs aided psychiatric professionals in this transition. In the 1950s, asylums were portrayed in the media as "snake pits," and the U.S. resident patient census was at its peak, 558,922 (Morrissey, 1982). It was not until the 1960s that the restructuring of mental health services was in full swing.

In 1961, the Joint Commission on Mental Illness and Health issued a report, *Action for Mental Health,* calling for the deinstitutionalization of the mentally ill. It emphasized the debilitating effects of hospitalization on the mentally ill and called for the establishment of community-based treatment centers and for a halt to the construction of large state institutions. In 1963, the Mental Retardation Facilities and Community Mental Health Centers Construction Act was passed. This legislation authorized federal grants for building community-based clinics. Two years later, it was amended to help fund services.

This legislative initiative was encouraged by civil litigation during the 1960s and 1970s (Ennis, 1972). Early cases challenged the right of the state to commit those among the mentally ill who were merely "different." These court rulings led to stricter statutory definitions of "dangerousness to self or others" as the legal criteria for commitment. In 1969, California passed the Lanterman-Petris-Short Act, which formalized these more stringent criteria and established elaborate procedures for commitment. In the 1970s, nearly every other state in the country adopted similar legislation. In addition, civil litigation during these two decades established the right of mental patients to legal defense in all due process hearings and reviewed the conduct of hospital staff for violations of patients' civil liberties.

The imposition of legal standards and norms upon the state mental hospital changed the dynamic of the organization in several ways. For one thing, legal advocates for both the patient and the hospital entered the decision-making structure of the institution. As professionals with a vested interest in the new legal procedures that were being imposed upon the commitment process, lawyers challenged the medical authority that had previously controlled hospital care. These legal battles often placed the reform-minded lawyer in the position of directing hospital policy. In addition, the extension of civil rights to the mentally ill altered the relationship between patients and therapists. For instance, patients gained the right to request release from the hospital and to have their requests considered in court within five days. With this right, patients gained leverage in their negotiations with staff for release and drew legal personnel further into the clinical decision-making process.

Throughout this period, the state mental hospital began to open up to the involvement of a variety of interest groups. The asylum had been characterized primarily by its isolation from the surrounding community and its total control over the lives and egos of its inmates (Goffman, 1961). In the 1960s, however, innovative administrators began to claim that the isolation of the hospital from the surrounding community was creating unnecessary distrust and misunderstanding between those inside and outside the mental institution (Greenblatt, Sharaf, & Stone, 1971). In addition, it was argued that the hospital could benefit from the resources of the community by opening its doors to enthusiastic volunteers and students. Therefore, hospital staff who had once lived on hospital grounds were now told to live in the community, and programs were designed to encourage the input of local interests in the life of the hospital. Greenblatt, York, and Brown (1955) and Greenblatt et al. (1971) wrote about changes at Boston State Hospital during this period.

> Although Boston State did not have a large live-in staff population, there were still enough to make the philosophy of living out a controversial issue. . . . Not only did this liberate the staff from the insularity of hospital life, but it also freed space—without disrupting patients—to bring more of the outside world into the hospital, especially in the form of independently financed research projects and university-affiliated programs. Thus, several floors of one attractive building were vacated and the space converted into offices for research personnel. Eventually, living quarters in three other buildings were emptied, thereby releasing even more room to establish working areas for personnel connected with new programs. (Greenblatt et al., 1971, p. 25)

Changes in the operation of the state mental hospital, like the penitentiary, were the result, in part, of the influx of new actors into the organizational structure. Mental health workers, for instance, like other state workers, were unionized. The union not only negotiated with hospital administrators issues such as salary and benefits, it also provided representation for staff members when grievances were lodged against them. The control of the administration over the staff of the hospital became regulated by formal standards that prohibited brutality against patients and procedures by which staff who violated these rules could be separated only after due process and contractual guarantees were protected. One of the effects of unionization upon the state hospital was that the traditional authority mechanisms of the hospital administration were limited in favor of a more pluralistic form of management involving several layers of decision makers.

Not only has the decision-making structure of the institution changed, but the treatment of patients is now a more open process in which the hospital and its staff compose only one of many agencies involved in the care of the mentally ill. As the hospital became more open to the participation of outside parties in its operation, the structure of the hospital began to change to accommodate other agencies in the treatment process. Reformers of the 1960s challenged the medical model that had characterized the structure of the hospital until that time. Proponents of milieu therapy stressed the importance of environment on the inception and the course of a person's mental illness. This new philosophy provided a theoretical basis for the reorganization of the hospital into therapeutic teams, which consisted of psychiatric, social work, and custodial staff who shared responsibility for the treatment and placement of their patients.

Before long, therapeutic teams were organized into treatment units that served geographical areas. Perrucci (1974) pointed out the significance of the reorganization of the mental hospital in conjunction with the precepts of milieu therapy. It broke down the isolation of the asylum and encouraged interaction between hospital staff and others involved in the life of the patients. Initially, this meant that families became more involved in the clinical decisions that therapists made. In planning discharge, staff might persuade family members to allow a patient to return home, thus facilitating his or her release. On the other hand, family members might prolong hospitalization by resisting the patient's return. The interaction of staff with those outside the hospital eventually extended to a whole network of social service agencies.

Recent analyses of the mental health system have shown that it has both expanded and fragmented. Smaller, increasingly private facilities treat a growing proportion of the mentally ill in a process that has been called "transinstitutionalism" in the mental health literature (Warren, 1981). As has been the case with both adult and juvenile correctional facilities, the changes in the utilization of the state mental hospital have been more than offset by the increase in the number of people who come in contact with one of these agencies (Cohen, 1985; Lerman, 1982; Warren, 1981). In addition, social service systems are more closely interconnected as clients move in and out of jails, halfway houses, welfare programs, and the state mental hospital.

Several studies (Gruenberg & Archer, 1979; Reich, 1973) have documented that welfare agencies have taken over some of the responsibilities of the state mental hospital. Indeed, as a policy of short-term hospitalization became accepted in state facilities throughout the country, the task of mental health workers has become one of arranging a variety of social service referrals for the mentally ill. For instance, hospital staff now try to find housing for their patients. This effort requires contact with halfway houses, temporary shelters, and landlords. In addition, patients often come to the hospital with problems with the Department of Welfare or in need of Social Security disability payments. Hospital staff help the mentally ill navigate these bureaucracies.

As the organizational structure of the state mental hospital has changed, so has the relationship between the staff of that institution and the mentally ill. Goffman (1961) described the means by which the "total" institution created the "self" of its inmates. With the hospital providing the only source of self-definition for the patient and labeling every act of rebellion—such as silence or insolence—as mental illness, the patient took on an institutionalized persona. The institution now holds few patients for long periods of time. The average duration of care in the state mental hospital declined from over twenty years in 1950 to seven months in 1979; the great majority of patients now are treated for no longer than sixty days (Redlich & Kellert, 1978). With the restructuring of the state hospital to encourage interaction between staff and the patient's family, not to mention other advocates, the institution became less dominant and the patient was presented with multiple definitions of self. When the institution was opened to varying pressures from outside parties, the hospital staff altered its relationship to the patients. When families and other agencies became involved in the care of the mentally ill, psychiatric personnel lost pervasive control over the fate and therefore the definition of self of their clients.

Patients now spend much more of their lives in their communities. According to Talbott (1984), most mental patients spend only 5 percent of their lives in the mental hospital, although 10–15 percent still spend more than half their lives there. The role of the mentally ill in their community, their economic status, whether or not they live with their families, their personality, and their definitions of their illness are now more than ever factors that affect the quality of patients' lives and the utilization of mental health services.

The "total institution" defined the economic, social, and psychiatric aspects of patients' lives. By definition, the total institution controlled every aspect of the self. Today's mental hospital is another matter. Patients are in and out after short stays. Their material needs for food and shelter are only very temporarily met by the hospital. After a week or two, the patients of state mental hospitals must once again struggle to pay the rent, work out conflictual relationships, pay for food, find busfare. The differences among patients, in terms of economic status and social support, take on increasing significance in the discussion of how to help mental patients in an era of deinstitutionalization. Their utilization of mental health services and the quality of their lives depend on a variety of factors besides their psychoses.

The Declining Significance of Mental Illness

The dilemma of mental illness looks quite different from the perspective we are developing. In order to address the problems that the mentally ill currently face, we must move beyond the deinstitutionalization debate, in which this policy is viewed as the primary cause of homelessness, poverty, and readmission. The policy of deinstitutionalization is only one aspect of a radical transformation that has occurred in a variety of social institutions. The admission and discharge practices of the state mental hospital have been blamed for the contemporary problems of the mentally ill. And yet, the authority of the hospital itself has become quite limited.

In this new world, it is not so much one's diagnosis that determines where one is treated and for how long, but rather one's economic status and personal goals. This fact has been substantiated by research on the impact of deinstitutionalization upon the mentally ill. For instance, several critics have talked about poor conditions in nursing homes and board-and-care facilities in which many of the mentally ill live (Bassuk & Gerson, 1978; Schmidt, Richardson, & Kane, 1977; Shadish, Straw, McSweeney, Koller, & Bootzin, 1981). Others have documented homelessness among the mentally ill (Lipton, Sabatini, & Katz, 1983). Some of these commentators have called for a form of "reinstitutionalization" in which state facilities would regain greater responsibility for the mentally ill (Arnhoff, 1975). Others have criticized the low rate at which treatment programs have been established in the community (Bassuk & Gerson, 1978).

However, there is some evidence that these problems of poor housing and homelessness depend less on patients' psychoses than on their economic status. Lehman, Ward, and Linn (1982) demonstrated the economic roots of the quality of mental patients' lives when they found that mental patients were significantly less satisfied than the general population in five areas (finances, employment, safety, family, and social relations). However, when compared to other "underprivileged" groups, the differences were less dramatic. In addition, a wide range of studies have shown that a variety of factors besides mental relapse contribute to hospital readmission; these include personality, family involvement, marital status, and community characteristics (Blumenthal, Kreisman, & O'Connor, 1982; Franklin, Kittredge, & Thrasher, 1975; Greenley, 1979; Segal & Aviram, 1979).

However, there are few data that describe the role of the state mental hospital in the lives of the deinstitutionalized mental patient or the process by which social and economic factors affect rehospitalization. Rosenblatt and Mayer (1974) argued that in today's mental health system many patients rationally weigh their options and decide to seek readmission. Lewis and Hugi (1981) substantiated this perspective when they found that mental patients returned to the hospital for both shelter and social support. Less well-documented is the extent to which financial limitations or other factors prevent the mentally ill from seeking out the resources of the mental health system despite the presence of symptomology.

It is likely that, for the very poor, a serious disease leads to a dependent status and minimal levels of care in private and public institutions. While the possibilities for care are manifold, the lack of personal resources and the potential for receiving welfare (SSI, SSDI, AFDC, GA, etc.) lead to a reliance on public programs. For those with resources, many options for care are available; these can be shaped by what the person wants and where he or she decides to get it. In other words, the human service market works for those who can afford to shop and who desire the products on sale.

The mentally ill underclass has been hurt most by the integration of the mentally ill into the mainstream of American society because this group is least capable of taking advantage of new treatment opportunities. When modern critics speak of the problems of the current system such as frequent readmissions, the homeless mentally ill, or the young chronic, they are speaking of the mentally ill who do not have the resources to make use of the integrated system. These persons are not "falling through the cracks," as some would like to argue. Rather, they lack the resources to make use of their new integrated status. Ironically, more services, more litigation, and improved specification of their emotional problems will not solve the problem, for these do not address the issue that keeps them poorly served. They simply lack the income and the associated values that would lead them to avail themselves of the services and other options of the new system (Rainwater, 1974). This class inequality, which the poor mentally ill share with many others, is the root of current policy dilemmas.

Conclusion

Once, the asylum was the focus of mental health policy discussion. The state mental hospital segregated the mentally ill for relatively long segments of their lives. In order to improve the quality of these lives, the procedures of the state mental hospital and the practices of its staff had to be addressed. Ultimately, the structure of the institution itself was attacked by policy analysts even before the 1960s and 1970s. Some have continued to debate the policy of deflection (turning people away from the hospital) and short-term hospitalization, which has been called "deinstitutionalization," as though the custodial institution still exists. For instance, Treffert (1974) argues that patients are "dying with their rights on." The authority of the state mental hospital to treat the mentally ill should be restored in some form.

But the contemporary state mental hospital has been altered by a historical process that has swept through social service systems and institutions of social control. Legal reform and the integration of institutions such as the penitentiary and the state mental hospital have altered the decision-making structure and relations between staff and inmates. As the rule of law reached inside the hospital, so did the concern of groups who sought better care for the mentally ill. Patient advocates began to ask that humane treatment be given and that state hospitals be open to scrutiny. Scholars began to represent the patients' perspective as they saw it. The hospital was penetrated by many new groups, from government officials to media personnel. The central institutions of the society, concerned about the regulation of social control agencies, became involved in their operation. Federal agencies were created to rationalize national policy toward the mentally ill as the federal government began to accept responsibility for financing part of that care and protecting its recipients from its excesses.

As this was occurring, funding shifted to some degree to smaller facilities, both public and private. The effect was to expand the reach of services and increase the number of clients served. The traditional institutions that had been responsible for the mentally ill, juveniles, and adult criminals are now interconnected with nontraditional agencies and each other as clients move around a network of public and private social services.

With this transformation, the state mental hospital has come to play a very different role in the lives of mental patients. The focus of policy analysis, we have argued, must be deinstitutionalized as well. The lives of patients, as they negotiate this complex service network, must be studied. Efforts at reform must now be focused on the community, where the mentally ill spend most of their lives struggling with economic and personal issues. Problems of poverty, homelessness, and domestic conflict among the mentally ill can no longer be blamed on the policy of deinstitutionalization. The issue of economic dependency itself must be confronted before the state mental patient can be effectively integrated into the community.

Similar conclusions have been reached in the study of the penitentiary. In his introduction to Jacobs's (1977) study of the penitentiary, Janowitz indicated the direction reform must take after the institution has been changed.

The rule of law can at best create the preconditions for effective programs of rehabilitation and social education. But juridical review cannot guarantee them an effective right, because there is not a foundation of knowledge on which to base such programs. At best, the juridical intrusion into the prison serves to permit the responsible penetration of external groups into the life of the prison and to increase the likelihood of contacts between the inmates and the agencies of the larger civil society. Attaining the major goal of reducing the size of the prisoner population depends not on prison reform but on a fundamental transformation of the agencies of education and employment which manage the transition from youth to adult status. (Jacobs, 1977, p. xii)

As Janowitz pointed out, the economic and social issues now faced by deinstitutionalized inmates in their communities must be confronted.

The inclusion of the mentally ill into the polity has not addressed the social isolation of those among them who are poor and dependent. For citizenship to have meaning, one must have the resources to make use of that individual freedom. Given the changes in our Chicago economy and labor markets, the very poorest among us are not able to maintain an independent existence. The question society has to face is whether their plight is severe enough and poses enough of a threat to our central institutions that we must again reach out and incorporate those outside the economic franchise. Conventional discussions of deinstitutionalization cast current problems as failures of reform commitment or imagination. Those problems are more the result of integrating the social control function with the central institutions of the society and the economy. The irony is that our commitment to individualism integrates the mentally ill in such a way as to make the poorest among them both freer and more dependent at the same time.

3 A PROFILE OF THE STATE MENTAL PATIENT

Mental health policy, to be effective, must be based on an accurate understanding of the mentally ill. This chapter describes the people who enter state mental hospitals in Chicago. The descriptions are based on data from three sources. First, the Mental Health Policy Project of Northwestern University's Center for Urban Affairs and Policy Research conducted a survey of 313 randomly selected patients who entered the four state hospitals serving Chicago. The patients were interviewed while still in the hospital, usually just prior to their release. In addition to undergoing a diagnostic assessment—the Schedule for Affective Disorders and Schizophrenia (SADS)— conducted by independent clinicians, patients were questioned for over an hour about their current hospitalization, the factors associated with it, and the kind of help they had received prior to admission. Second, with the assistance of the Chicago Police Department, we ascertained the criminal histories of the entire sample, including recent arrest reports. Finally, the Illinois Department of Mental Health and Developmental Disabilities (DMH) supplied information about the previous treatment histories of the patients.

Two-thirds of the patients in the sample are male, well over half are black, and the overwhelming majority are without work and on welfare. Only 6.7 percent of the sample takes in over $12,000 per year. Sixty-three percent of the patients are not visiting the hospital for the first time; black women lead all other demographic groups in recidivism, over 38 percent of them having had six or more previous admissions.

Eighty percent of the sample is diagnosed as either schizophrenic or manic-depressive. Hospital staff diagnosed 14 percent more people schizophrenic than did the independent diagnosticians. Black males are diagnosed schizophrenic more often than any other group of patients by both hospital and independent clinicians.

Fewer than half of the sample received treatment or counseling before being admitted to the hospital. For those who did receive help before they were admitted, that help typically consisted of seeing a professional twice during the two months prior to admission, for less than an hour each time. This help focused on their medication. Despite their extremely low incomes, many had no help with their money, job, health, or personal problems before their admission, suggesting that the hospital may be the first, rather than the last, service for many when emotional problems become severe. Those who did receive some help were aided by a relative; public aid was the only public agency used with any frequency by the sample.

In our sample, less than 3 percent of the admissions to Chicago-area state facilities result from involuntary commitments, whereas 97 percent of the sample were voluntary admissions. While this transformation to a voluntary system suggests a less coercive role for the hospital, it also suggests that patients who pose a threat to society are no longer under court supervision. Indeed, our data suggest that those who pose a threat to society are no more likely to be involuntarily committed than less dangerous patients. Additionally, the state's reliance on voluntary admission circumvents the legal protections enjoyed by those who are involuntarily committed.

Thirty-four percent of the sample had been arrested from 1 to 55 times prior to their hospitalization. Thirty-eight percent of the prior arrests with known dispositions had resulted in convictions; 97 of the patients out of the sample of 313 had been sentenced to jail or prison terms arising from convictions for nearly 150 separate charges. Fifteen percent of the sample was arrested within twelve months after their hospitalization, most commonly for municipal or petty crimes, e.g., loitering, disorderly conduct, public intoxication, and traffic offenses.

Patients come to the hospitals for various reasons. Some seek treatment voluntarily. Some are brought, against their will, by the police; others are brought to the hospital by concerned family members. Some are sent back to the hospital by other service agencies.

Table 3–1 describes our sample. Table 3–2 compares the sample with the total hospital population (the universe we sought to reproduce) and shows that, with the exception of a significant and planned bias in our sample toward patients with six or more previous admissions, the sample represents that population quite well. But table 3–1 also tells a story in itself. Chicago-area state hospitals primarily serve young adult males, who make up more than 60 percent of the patients in all the hospitals. When we look to the

Table 3–1. The MHPP* Sample: Demographics by Admitting Facility

	Admitting Facility									
	Read		*Madden*		*Tinley*		*ISPI*		*Total*	
	%	N	%	N	%	N	%	N	%	N
Sex										
Male	65	85	62	48	67	40	56	25	63	198
Female	35	45	38	29	34	21	44	20	37	115
Race										
Black	33	43	63	47	84	51	66	31	55	173
White	54	70	32	24	10	6	20	9	35	109
Hispanic	9	11	3	2	1	2	7	3	5	17
Asian	2	3	1	1	0	0	2	1	2	4
Other	2	3	1	1	5	2	7	1	3	3
Age										
18–34	65	80	65	51	74	45	71	32	67	209
35–49	27	35	23	15	18	11	18	8	23	72
50–65	10	13	12	9	8	5	11	5	10	32
Previous Admissions										
0	38	44	38	24	30	18	47	21	37	117
1–5	33	43	33	25	30	18	29	13	31	97
6+	29	38	30	23	40	25	24	11	32	99
Totals	42	130	24	77	19	61	14	45	100	313

*The Mental Health Policy Project Sample refers to the panel survey of state patients collected for this study.

north-side facility (Read), we see a racial composition different from that of the rest of the facilities. Whites comprise half the admissions at Read, which contributes 42 percent of the total admissions, while blacks on average comprise over 70 percent of all the admissions at the other facilities. Two-thirds of all admissions are males under 35. Chicago is a segregated city, so its state hospital populations have very different racial compositions.

As one reads down each column in table 3–1, the differences among hospitals emerge. Tinley Park admits patients with long histories of state hospitalization (40 percent), even though it has the

Table 3–2. Comparing the Wave 1 Sample with a Population of Mental Patients, July 1, 1983–December 31, 1984

	Wave 1 Respondents (N=313)	Patient Population (N=10,133)	Statistical Test for Differences
	MHPP	DMH	
Sex			
Male	63.3%	60.7%	$\chi^2 (1)=.871$
Female	36.7	39.3	ns
Race			
Black	55.3	58.9	$\chi^2 (2)=2.32$
White	34.8	33.1	ns
Other	10.0	8.0	
Age			
18–34	66.7	61.4	$\chi^2 (2)=3.76$
35–49	23.0	26.6	ns
50–65	10.2	12.0	
Previous Admissions			
0	37.4	41.6	$\chi^2 (2)=12.78$
1–5	31.6	36.0	$p<.01$
6+	31.0	22.4	

highest proportion of young admittees. In contrast, Read has many admittees (38 percent) who have never been to the hospital before, even though it has the highest proportion of middle-aged admissions (27 percent). Moreover, it has a larger percentage of women than any of the other hospitals.

When we look at the people, rather than the facilities, a picture of both the common features and differences emerges. State mental patients share some general characteristics but at the same time fall into distinct subgroups. Since their heterogeneity has a profound effect on patients' experiences, we focus on that here, and categorize the patients according to their gender and race: white males, white females, black males, black females, and others. The "others" category, consisting of Hispanics, Asians, and other ethnic groups, contained too few people to allow separate subgroup analyses. Table

Table 3–3. The MHPP Sample: Gender/Race Categories

	Percent of Total Sample	Number of Respondents
White males	22.0	69
White females	12.8	40
Black males	34.5	108
Black females	20.8	65
Other	9.9	31
Totals	100	313

3–3 presents the proportion of each category in the whole sample. We can look at both differences and similarities in these categories of patients.

Urban state mental patients are, for the most part, young, male, black, and poor. Only 21 (6.7 percent) of the patients' incomes exceed $1,000 per month, and most of those are white males. An examination of the distribution of income illustrates this point further. The average income of the sample (excluding missing observations) was approximately $407 per month. The median income, a more accurate reflection of sample income, was just $300 per month. Furthermore, eighteen (6.6 percent) individuals in the sample reported no monthly income, and another 19.6 percent reported $100 or less per month.

Table 3–4 further illustrates the point by showing that at least two-thirds of the patients in all demographic subgroups were not employed two months prior to hospitalization. Approximately 40 percent of the entire sample had no money from work to pay their bills prior to hospitalization.

The data (table 3–5) revealed the overwhelming economic dependence of mental hospital patients. Over 60 percent of the black patients report they receive public aid, and about half also get aid from their families. Over one-half of whites report aid from their families, and white males (58 percent) report more welfare dependency than females (35 percent).

Besides being jobless and highly dependent upon public aid, the state patients also are quite transient (table 3–6). Many have moved

Table 3–4. The MHPP Sample: Gender/Race by Previous Employment and Money from Job

	Not Previously (2 Months) Employed	No Money from Job to Pay Bills
White males	66.7%	48.6%
White females	65.5	47.4
Black males	65.7	42.1
Black females	83.1	66.7
Other	80.6	76.5
Total N	223	83

Table 3–5. The MHPP Sample: Sources of Financial Aid

	Family		Public Aid		Total
	Number	%	Number	%	Number
White males	24	34.8	40	58.0	69
White females	22	55.0	14	35.0	40
Black males	36	33.3	68	63.0	108
Black females	17	26.2	42	64.4	65
Other	17	54.8	10	32.3	31
Total	116	37.1	174	55.6	313

often, some are homeless, and others reside frequently in the hospital. Adequate housing remains a problem for many: over 31 percent of the patients suggested that they had "a great deal" of worry over a place to stay.

The respondents were asked how many times they had moved in the last six months. Some 41.9 percent stated that they had moved at least once during the previous six months. Some 35.5 percent of the sample had moved from one to three times, while 6.4 percent had moved up to nine times. Table 3–6 indicates that blacks were a more stably housed group than whites. Of the four groups, white males are the most transient.

Table 3–6.   The MHPP Sample: Gender/Race by Number of Residential Moves in Last Six Months

	Zero	Moved at Least Once	Total N
White males	46.4%	53.6%	69
White females	52.5	47.5	40
Black males	63.0	37.0	108
Black females	67.7	32.3	65
Other	54.8	45.2	31
Total N	182	131	313

Most of the patients in the sample are not visiting the hospital for the first time (table 3–7). According to Department of Mental Health (DMH) statistics, 62.6 percent of the sample had been admitted previously to the state system; roughly half of these had been admitted six or more times. Of those with six or more admissions, black females make up the largest proportion, with black males not too far behind.

Turning to table 3–8, it can be seen that the overwhelming majority of the males are under 35 years of age (62.3 percent of white males and 81.5 percent of black males). We are confronted with a

Table 3–7.   The MHPP Sample: Number of Previous Hospitalizations

	None		1 to 5		6 or More		Total
	#	%	#	%	#	%	Number
White males	20	29.0	30	43.5	19	27.5	69
White females	19	47.5	13	32.5	8	20.0	40
Black males	37	34.3	33	30.6	38	35.2	108
Black females	27	41.5	13	20	25	38.5	65
Other	14	45.2	10	32.3	7	22.6	31
Total	117	37.4	99	31.6	97	31.0	313

Table 3–8. The MHPP Sample: Gender/Race by Age

	18 to 35	35 to 49	50 Plus	Total N
White males	62.3%	30.4%	7.2%	69
White females	50.0	32.5	17.5	40
Black males	81.5	15.7	2.8	108
Black females	50.8	30.8	18.5	65
Other	80.0	3.2	16.1	31
Total N	209	72	32	313

young male population that is economically dependent. Given that black males constitute 34.5 percent of the sample and white males another 22 percent, these young men have the highest state hospital utilization rates for Chicagoans.

White females stand out in the sample in a variety of ways. First, while they are as poor as other groups, more of them are high school graduates. Furthermore, white women have better familial support systems, as evidenced by their overall better economic status and less dependency on public aid. White women are also more likely to be married and to have lower readmission rates. Finally, white females are less likely than any of the other groups to be diagnosed as schizophrenic.

White males live alone more than any other group and are more likely to have been previously hospitalized. Of those who have been married, white males have the greatest incidence of divorce. Furthermore, more of them perceive hospitalization a result of lifestyle problems (e.g., drug and alcohol use) than do members of other groups.

The black female group exhibits the highest frequency of those on public assistance. This fact is obviously related to its being the poorest group in the sample. Most of these women live with someone else, yet report the lowest levels of receiving familial aid.

Black males reside with adult relatives (most of these are parents). Black males are more commonly single and also have the highest high school dropout rate of the four groups. Black males are the youngest group and also have higher rates of readmission than the other groups. Furthermore, more black males perceive themselves

Table 3–9. The MHPP Sample: Education

| | High School Education | | | | Total |
| | Not Completed | | Completed | | |
	Number	%	Number	%	Number
White males	29	42.0	40	58.0	69
White females	14	35.0	26	65.0	40
Black males	55	50.9	53	49.1	108
Black females	29	44.6	36	55.4	65
Other	22	71.0	9	29.0	31
Total	149	47.6	164	52.4	313

as having no significant problems than any other group in the sample.

In this sample, nearly half—47.6 percent—had not completed high school (table 3–9). White women most frequently completed their high school education. In the major gender and race groupings, white females appeared to be the most likely to be married. The highest incidence of divorce occurred in the white male grouping at 76.5 percent. Every other group's rate was less than half of this.

The majority of respondents in the sample resided with another individual. Table 3–10 shows that whites resided alone considerably more than blacks. Most black males were single and living with a parent.

Help Prior to Admission

Over one-third (36 percent) of the patients in this study had never before been admitted to a psychiatric hospital; the remaining two-thirds had one or more admissions and were eligible for aftercare services. In addition to aftercare, patients might have received help from family, friends, or other acquaintances. We examined help-seeking behavior by asking the patients whether they had received help before they were admitted to the hospital. They were also asked to identify "the first person or organization you went to

Table 3–10. The MHPP Sample: Living Arrangements

	Living Alone		Living with Someone		Total
	Number	%	Number	%	Number
White males	32	47.8	35	52.2	67
White females	12	32.4	25	67.6	37
Black males	24	23.5	76	76.5	102
Black females	12	19.4	50	80.6	62
Other	9	29.0	22	71.0	31
Total	89	29.8	210	70.2	299

for help the last time you had a money problem, housing problem, job problem, health problem, or personal problem." Finally, they were asked to "imagine you felt yourself getting upset or feeling bad. Do you know some organization or person that you would go to for help? [If yes] What person or organization would you go to?" While most previous research on help seeking looks at medical problems, we wanted to see whether there was a general pattern in help seeking that obtained regardless of problem, or whether this population used different resources for different types of problems. We looked not only at the use of psychiatric services, but also at the use of a variety of public and private sources of help (e.g., public aid, private charities, loan companies, etc.).

Professional Help Immediately Prior to Hospital Admission

For some, hospital admission may be the last step in a series of attempts to get help. A person may seek out relatives, friends, or professionals before going to the hospital. We do not have information about people who sought help and successfully stayed out of the hospital, but we did ask patients in our sample, "In the two months before you entered the hospital, were you seeing anyone for treatment or counseling or going to a self-help group?" Overall,

Table 3–11. The MHPP Sample: Type of Person Seen for Counseling or Treatment in Two Months Prior to Hospital Admission

Person Seen	Number of Patients	Percent
No one	166	55.1
Medical doctor	15	5.0
Psychiatrist	65	21.6
Other mental health professional	38	12.6
Self-help group	6	2.0
Other	11	3.7

54.5 percent of the sample responded no to this question, while 45.5 percent said yes. There were no significant differences in response to this question by race, sex, education, or income. There *were* differences by age: those who were older were more likely to be seeing someone (χ^2=10.27, df=2, p=.01). While this may simply be an artifact (those who have lived longer have had more opportunity to become connected to a professional caregiver), it may also indicate that the younger patients, who now make up the bulk of the hospital population, do not have access to or do not make use of available alternative services.

Since those who have been admitted to the hospital previously have had the benefit of a referral to a community agency, we might expect that those with more previous admissions would be more likely to have seen someone for help before entering the hospital. There is a trend in that direction, but it does not reach statistical significance.

We asked those who did see someone for help who it was they saw, how often they saw that person, and, each time they saw him or her, about how much time was spent. Tables 3-11 and 3-12 show responses to these questions. Among those who did receive professional help, the most frequent (21.6 percent) source of that help was a psychiatrist. Only six people in this sample availed themselves of a self-help group, a source of help that has become increasingly popular among other groups with problems in living. The most frequent answer to the question of how often a provider of help was

Table 3–12. The MHPP Sample: Frequency of Contact with Counselor/Other in Two Months Prior to Hospital Admission

Frequency	Number of Patients	Percent
Less than 1/month	9	7.1
1/month	41	32.3
2/month	20	15.7
1/week	29	22.8
More than 1/week	28	22.0

seen was once a month, and the length of time spent in those meetings averaged 48.7 minutes. Thus, people who did receive professional help in the two months prior to hospitalization typically saw a psychiatrist twice, for less than an hour each time. While, as stated above, those whose help-seeking efforts enabled them to stay out of the hospital were not a part of this sample, those who entered the hospital appear to have received little professional help just prior to that admission.

When we asked people what type of treatment they received during these sessions, the most common answer (47.1 percent) was medication or a combination of medication and therapy; the next most common answer was individual therapy (36.7 percent).

Finally, we asked if those receiving professional help had also received help with practical problems, such as money or housing. About 64 percent of the sample had not received such help; of those who did, the most frequent type of help was public assistance. Given the likely relationship between housing problems and rehospitalization for at least some of this sample, the fact that only 9 people out of the sample of 313 had received help with housing is particularly salient.

When we asked those who sought help but had not received it what had happened, the most frequent response (42.9 percent) was that they had been referred to the hospital.

In sum, the typical picture of help received from mental health professionals in the two months before entering the hospital appears as follows: fewer than half the patients received any professional help; those who did receive help saw a psychiatrist twice during this period, for less than an hour each time, and received help mostly concerning medication. They received little help with practical problems. Finally, referral to the hospital was a common response when people sought help. Thus, resources for diverting people from the hospital in the two months before admissions do not seem to be reaching this patient group.

Problem-Solving Efforts Prior to Hospitalization

Professional caregivers may be only one among an array of sources of help sought by psychiatric patients prior to hospital admission. We asked people to identify the person or organization they went to for help the last time they had a money problem, housing problem, job problem, health problem, or personal problem. The following discussion addresses each type of problem separately, and examines first the use of organizations as sources of help, and then people. Finally, we examine overall patterns of help seeking among demographic subgroups, considering both people and organizations as sources of help.

MONEY PROBLEM

We asked patients in our sample from whom they sought help the last time they had a money problem, giving them the opportunity to identify both a person and an organization as sources of help. While only 14 people of 313 (about 4 percent) reported that they had had no money problems, only 84 people (about 27 percent) reported using an organization as a source of aid. About half of those identified public aid or Social Security as the source of help, while another 25 percent used a private charity. Differences appeared by race (but not other demographic criteria) in organizations used as sources of help: 71.1 percent of blacks used public aid or Social Security, while only 38.2 percent of whites did so. Only 2.2 percent of blacks used loan companies, while 20.6 percent of whites did. In sum, whites used mostly private sources of aid, while blacks were more likely to use public sources.

When we examined those people used for help during a money problem, the most common source was a parent (37.8 percent) or other family member (35.1 percent). While there were no differences by race, gender, education, income, previous admission, or diagnosis in the types of persons used for help, differences did appear by age: 49 percent of those 18–24 years old used a parent as a source of help, while only 20.7 percent of those 35–49 did so. About 59 percent of the latter used other family members, while only 27 percent of the former did so. Obviously, this could be an artifact, since fewer older people have parents living who could be sources of help.

The most common source of help with money problems is a relative. While 49 people used public aid or Social Security, more than twice as many (108) used a parent or other relative. In accordance with previous research, relatives provide tangible aid such as money more frequently than friends.

HOUSING PROBLEM

Since about 18 percent of the sample considered housing problems one of the reasons for their hospitalization, identifying sources of support for housing problems is particularly important in reducing the frequency of rehospitalizations. Organizational help for housing problems was most frequently (about 55 percent) provided by a charity, social service, or mental health agency. Of those who used an organization for help, about 17.3 percent of the people in our sample said they had used a shelter the last time they had a housing problem (table 3–13).

When we examined sources used for help with housing problems by demographic subgroups, several differences appeared. First, when we considered organizations used as sources of help, differences appeared by age, income, race, and number of previous admissions. The relationship between income and organizations used for help is as one might expect: the more money one has, the less likely one is to use a shelter. (The comparison here is between those with an income less than $3,000 per year vs. those with $3,001–$6,000 per year.) Those with more money are more likely to use a charity or social service agency. Those who are older (35–49 years old) are also more likely to use a charity or social service agency than a shelter. About 33.3 percent of people in this age group used a charity or social service agency, as compared to 4.2 percent who used a shelter. Among the younger group, about 23 percent used a shelter, compared to 29.2 percent who used a social service agency.

Differences by race and number of previous admissions also ap-

Table 3–13. The MHPP Sample: Use of Organizations for Help with Housing by Number of Previous Admissions

	0	1–5	6+	Fre-quency	Per-cent
Public aid	6 (24.0)*	2 (9.5)	2 (6.9)	10	13.3
Shelter	6 (24.0)	3 (14.3)	4 (13.8)	13	17.3
Charity, social service agency	6 (24.0)	6 (28.6)	12 (41.4)	24	32.0
Community organization	0 (0.0)	3 (14.3)	2 (6.9)	5	6.7
Private agency	1 (4.0)	1 (4.8)	4 (13.8)	6	8.0
Mental health agency	6 (24.0)	6 (28.6)	5 (17.1)	17	22.7
Total	25	21	29	75	100

*Numbers in parentheses indicate column percentages.

pear. More whites made use of a shelter than blacks (24.1 percent vs. 10.5 percent), while more blacks used a charity or social service agency than whites (36.8 percent vs. 27.6 percent). Table 3–14 presents the use of organizations for help with housing problems, by number of previous admissions. The more previous admissions, the less likely people were to say that housing was no problem. While

Table 3–14. The MHPP Sample: Persons Used for Help with Housing Problems

	Frequency	Percent
Parent	48	40.3
Other family	41	34.5
Friend	19	16.0
Professional	5	9.2
Total	119	100.0

overall the most likely source of help is a charity or social service agency, the use of this source of help increases with more previous admissions.

Parents and other family members were by far the most frequent source of help with housing (table 3–14). Breakdown by demographic characteristics identified several differences among subgroups. First, blacks are more likely than whites to use parents for housing help (43.2 percent vs. 33.3 percent; while whites also use family most frequently, they are more likely to use a friend than blacks (25.6 percent vs. 10.8 percent). Males are most likely to use a parent (47.8 percent) or other family member (27.5 percent). While females also make most use of family, they are most likely to use other family members (48.7 percent) and then parents (25.6 percent). Age differences follow an expected pattern: overall, family members are the people most often called upon for help, but those who are younger resort to parents most often, while older people turn to other family members most often.

Overwhelmingly, people appeal to relatives when in a housing crisis. Ten of the people in our sample used public aid for help, thirteen used a shelter, eighty-nine used a relative, and nineteen a friend. Thus, as with money problems, people most often seek help from relatives, rather than professional or public sources of aid.

JOB PROBLEM

At least two-thirds of the patients in our sample were not employed two months prior to hospitalization. When we asked which organization or person people had turned to the last time they had a job problem, we found that 22 (out of 313) said they had never had a job (14 of these 22, or 64 percent, were female). Thirty-two people said they had never had a job problem. Only ninety people (less than one-third of the sample) mentioned any organization that they would go to for help in this case; the organization mentioned most frequently was an employment agency.

The person most often mentioned as a source of help for job problems was oneself (mentioned by twenty-seven people); relatives were cited by twenty-three people and friends by fifteen people (table 3–15).

When we combine all possible sources of help for job problems, we find that, in contrast to the pattern found with money and housing

Table 3–15. The MHPP Sample: Persons Used for Help with Job Problems

	Frequency	Percent
Parent	14	25.9
Other family	9	16.7
Friend	15	27.8
Professional	16	29.6
Total	54	100.0

problems, relatives are not most frequently turned to. Instead, thirty-two people mentioned an employment agency, nineteen mentioned an employer, fifteen mentioned public aid, fifteen mentioned a friend, fourteen mentioned a parent, and nine mentioned other family members. This indicates that help is sought from relatives for job problems, much less than for housing and money problems.

HEALTH PROBLEM

The overwhelming majority of those who mentioned a resource when facing a health problem identified a hospital or clinic or specific health agency (table 3–16). Similarly, the person most often identified as the source of help was a medical professional. Relatives were next in frequency. Curiously, the proportion of people who would use a hospital for help with a health problem decreases with more hospital admissions (table 3–17). While 87.5 percent of those with no previous admissions would use a hospital, this proportion drops to 58.3 percent for those with six or more admissions.

PERSONAL PROBLEM

When we asked patients in our sample what organization or person they went to for help the last time they had a personal problem, the most frequent answers were a parent (41 mentions) or other family member (53 mentions). Professional advisors or mental health organizations were mentioned by sixty-one persons (table 3–18). The only difference between subgroups was that of age: people in all age

Table 3–16. The MHPP Sample: Sources of Help with Health Problems

Source of Help	Number	%
Organization		
Hospital or clinic	88	72.7
Mental health organization	19	15.7
Health agency	14	11.6
Total	121	100.0
Person		
Medical Professional	84	72.4
Social Worker	2	1.7
Relative	22	19.0
Other	6	5.2
God	2	1.7
Total	116	100.0

Table 3–17. The MHPP Sample: Organizations Used for Help with Health Problems by Number of Previous Admissions

Organization	Number of Previous Admissions			Frequency	Percent
	0	1–5	6+		
Hospital	42 (87.5%)	25 (67.6%)	21 (58.3%)	88	72.7
Health agency	4 (8.3%)	3 (8.1%)	7 (19.4%)	14	11.6
Mental health organization, shelter, self-help group	2 (4.2%)	9 (24.3%)	8 (22.2%)	19	15.7
Total	48 (100%)	37 (100%)	36 (100%)	121	100.0

Table 3–18. The MHPP Sample: Sources of Help with Personal Problems

Source of Help	Number	%
Organization		
Hospital or clinic	9	34.6
Mental health organization	14	53.8
Shelter	2	7.7
Self-help group	1	3.8
Total	26	
Person		
Parent	41	24.1
Other family member	53	31.2
Friend	29	17.1
Mental health professional	32	18.8
Other professional	15	8.8
Total	170	

groups were most likely to mention a relative, but those who were younger mentioned a parent more frequently and those who were older mentioned other family. As discussed above, this may simply be an artifact: those who are younger are more likely to have living parents from whom to seek help.

In sum, the last time people had these problems in living, *many of them received no help from any organization or person.* Those who did receive help were most likely to receive it from *a relative* for money, housing, and personal problems. While relatives were not the most frequent source of help for job problems, this finding must be viewed in the context of the high rate of joblessness of this population. The relatively low use of public agencies for help with problems, with perhaps the exception of public aid or Social Security, parallels the low use of social service agencies in general by low-income groups in Chicago (Cook, Jencks, Mayer, Constantino, & Popkin, 1986, p. 45). The high use of relatives for help by mental hospital patients suggests that the life crises faced by the patient become crises for the family as well. Reorienting current services from the individual to the family might be more effective in reaching

Table 3–19. The MHPP Sample: Person or Organization Anticipated as Source of Help if Patient Became Upset Again

	Frequency	Percent
Relative	54	31.3
Friend	12	6.9
Neighbor	1	.6
Doctor	9	5.2
Mental health professional	35	20.3
Clergy	7	4.1
Other	6	3.5
Church	4	2.3
Community mental health center	17	9.8
Mental hospital	14	8.1
Other hospital	4	2.3
Self-help group	9	5.2
Shelter	1	.6
Agency	21	2.5
Total	172	

the patient, since family seems to be the agent of help most frequently used even by those with considerable experience in the mental health system.

The data cited above identified sources of help that people used the last time they had a particular problem and in the two months prior to hospitalization. In order to assess the degree to which patients anticipate solving problems in the future that might lead to rehospitalization, we asked the following question: "Imagine you felt yourself getting upset or feeling bad. Do you know some organization or person that you would go to for help?" About 36 percent of our sample said no; about 64 percent said yes. There were no differences among demographic subgroups in responses to this question. We then asked, "What person or organization would you go to?" The responses are presented in table 3–19. While almost one-third of the sample would go to a relative, a similar proportion would go to a mental health professional or community mental health center.

About 8 percent saw returning to the hospital as their first course of action.

Finally, we were interested in how people met the person they would turn to for help, since we wanted some measure of how deeply embedded in the mental health system our patients were. Previous studies have found that use of mental health services depends heavily on the referral of other professionals or friends or relatives who are familiar with these services. Of all those mentioned as sources of help if the patient became upset again, about 42 percent were related to the mental health system in some way—that is, a professional or friend met through a mental health agency—while 58 percent were not connected to the mental health system.

This patient population is dominated by very poor young males who receive little help before admission. Given the population's non-utilization of supports outside the hospital, a return to the hospital is not surprising. It seems that they have few other places to go when problems appear. In the next chapter we explore the issue of readmissions and identify the correlates of returning to the hospital as a way of understanding both the lives of the mentally ill and the nature of our current mental health system.

4 THE PUZZLE OF READMISSIONS

The previous two chapters describe the transformation of the state hospital and the current profile of state hospital patients. Given a population with severe and often chronic illnesses, with few supports and little income, and an organization (the state hospital) whose mission is to return that group to the community as quickly as is clinically and morally possible, it is no wonder that two-thirds of the patient population will return to the hospital.

Readmissions are not the consequence of the system's failure to operate effectively. Rather, they are a routine consequence of the interaction between the needs of a population (the poor mentally ill) and the goals of an organization (state hospitals). With few treatment alternatives (private facilities) available outside the state hospitals, and patients, their families, and other governmental and social institutions in need of an agency to take responsibility for the care and control of the mentally ill person, it is no wonder that many patients return to the hospital. The real problem with readmissions is not that they are so common, but that we understand so little about them. The reason we know so little is that we use research designs to study readmissions that distort the problem literally beyond recognition.

If our analysis of the state hospital is correct in suggesting a dramatic change in the last twenty years as we moved from an exclusionary to an inclusionary system of care, then we should look at the question of readmissions and chronicity in ways that do not depend on guild innovationism and mental health exceptionalism to see the issue. Most discussions of readmissions that rely on retrospective analysis make two cardinal assumptions: first, following mental health exceptionalism, that the illness is the primary cause of the rehospitalization; and second, following guild innovationism, that the way to reduce the number of rehospitalizations is to create a new clinical service that will do a better job of maintaining the person in the community. Unfortunately, the last two decades of reform have not produced convincing evidence that either assumption is warranted. If the hospital has become a therapeutic station for those with mental illness and is oriented toward integrating the patient back into the service system as quickly as possible, then the problem of readmissions cannot be reduced to the presence of symptomology and cannot be ameliorated by the addition of new clinical programs, which may act as conduits back to the hospital rather than alternatives to it.

The conventional way to study readmissions is to define the problem in terms of previous admissions. Many scholars do this because they are operating within a theoretical framework that treats an admission to the state hospital as if it were the culmination of a psychiatric career or illness episode. Reviewing a patient's previous admissions permits identification of the correlates of the number of previous admissions by simply working with the case records of patients who have entered the state hospital. This kind of research is practical and efficient for it involves working with records that are usually on hand. The problem, of course, is that by relying on data collected retrospectively, the sample being used is often biased toward those who over a lifetime both survive and continue to rely on the state hospitals. Those who are not readmitted are excluded from the sample. As we will show, this kind of research distorts the reality of readmissions that occur in a shorter time period (say, one year) and literally reverses the findings produced by a research design that prospectively charts which patients are readmitted. This prospective approach is useful to policy-oriented researchers, for it relies on a panel that can be tracked over time, so we can better understand the activities of those who use the hospitals and those who do not. By looking forward, we can see how the clinical and social factors operating in the community affect the behavior of state patients.

It is important to demonstrate how retrospective studies distort the readmissions problem. Our findings emerged from analyses of Illinois Department of Mental Health records of 10,068 admissions to Chicago-area state psychiatric hospitals during an eighteen-month interval extending from July 1, 1983, to December 31, 1984. All data were extracted from the Inpatient Summary Person File (ISPF). As shown in table 4–1, six major mental health facilities were represented in the study's archival base. The vast majority of patients (89 percent) were admitted and treated at three of the centers (Read, Tinley Park, and Madden). Case files, which are developed at each

Table 4–1. The DMH Population*: Admissions to Six Treatment Centers, July 1, 1983–December 31, 1984

Facility	N	%
Read	3,657	36
Tinley Park	2,870	29
Madden	2,460	24
ISPI	605	6
Elgin	264	3
Manteno	212	2
Total	10,068	100%

*The Department of Mental Health Population refers to all patients treated at Chicago-area state hospitals for the period 7/1/83 to 12/31/84.

of the institutions and collected in Springfield, consist largely of data gathered as a matter of course whenever there is movement in the system (i.e., admission, transfer, or discharge). Our analyses of the data were both descriptive and interpretive. The aim of the descriptive analyses was to portray the population in terms of fundamental sociodemographic and patient treatment/status variables and to explore the bivariate relationships of those variables to outcome criteria or dependent measures that reflect the course of patients' number of previous admissions. Our interpretive analyses centered upon the statistical prediction of these criteria within a multivariate framework.

Number of Previous Admissions

Apart from their most recent admission, patients had been previously hospitalized in a state psychiatric facility on the average of four occasions. While 39 percent had no prior hospitalization, more than half (52 percent) of the population had at least one prior admission, and 5 percent showed fifteen or more past institutionalizations on their records. Table 4–2 summarizes previous admissions.

Table 4–2. The DMH Population: Previous Admissions

Number of Previous Admissions	N	%
0	3,957	39
1–5	3,703	37
6 or more	2,408	24
Total	10,068	100%

Sex. Overall, a greater percentage of males (61 percent) were admitted to state psychiatric facilities. The number of male admittees was more than 1.5 times the number of female admittees to the system. Nonetheless, the relative distributions of males and females within each of the "number of previous admissions" categories (0, 1–5, 6 or more) were approximately equal for the two groups. More specifically, among male and female admittees, there was essentially no difference in the percentage of patients institutionalized for the first time during the eighteen-month period and the percentage reflecting one to five prior hospitalizations. A difference did appear in the groups when comparing multiple admittees (more than six prior hospitalizations) to the other two categories, i.e., multiple admittees comprised a smaller percentage of the subsamples for both males (25 percent) and females (23 percent).

Race. The incidence of black admissions to the system is substantially higher (60 percent) than that of nonblack admissions, i.e., whites (32 percent), and Hispanics, Orientals, Asians, and Indians (8 percent) (Hispanics represented 86 percent of the "Other" group). Although blacks and whites appear in roughly equal proportions within each of the three previous-admissions categories, a difference appeared across the categories in the "Other" racial group. Multiple admissions are comparatively less prevalent among Hispanics, Orientals, Asians, and Indians. Only 15 percent of the "Other" group evidenced multiple admissions, but the percentages of multiple admissions for blacks and whites were 26 percent and 22 percent, respectively.

Age. The mean age of the patients at admission was approximately 34 years. Ages ranged from 18 to 65, with half of the admittees above and below the age of 31 (the median age). The greatest proportion of all admissions (61 percent) appeared in the 18–34 age range. As expected, within the youngest group of patients, there was a steady decrease across the number of previous-admissions categories, with only 19 percent showing multiple admissions. In contrast, within the middle age (35–49) and the eldest group (50+), patients are as likely to be first-time admittees as multiple admittees.

Marital Status. In general, unmarried persons were disproportionately represented in the population of admittees (885) when compared to the general population. Moreover, patients who were married at the time of admission were also less likely to have been previously hospitalized. Twenty-five percent of the unmarried subsample consisted of multiple admittees, compared to 19 percent of the subsample of married patients.

A series of standard, stepwise multiple regression analyses was employed to assess the strength of the investigation's sociodemographic and patient status/treatment variables as predictors of number of previous admissions. The analyses quantified the singular or independent relationship of each variable to the criteria by removing, i.e., controlling for, the confounding influences of the remaining factors. In addition, they provided tests of the combined usefulness of the variables in forecasting the dependent measure.

Variables were introduced into the regression equation in two blocks. The first block comprised the sociodemographic and patient treatment/history variables, while the second block entered "type of facility" as a set of dummy-coded variables representing the six Chicago-area institutions encompassed in our data set. Results of the regressions are presented in table 4–3, which displays the standardized regression coefficients (beta) associated with the predictor variables, the F-values emerging from statistical tests of the beta coefficients, the level of significance attained by the F-values (p) and the multiple correlation (R) between the predictors (at each succeeding step in the analyses) and the criteria. Only those factors achieving the conventional level of statistical significance (.05) are reported.

As illustrated in table 4–3, the strongest predictor of previous admissions is *age*. Other significant predictors include (in descending order of importance): *marital status*—married patients do not turn to the hospital as often as unmarried patients; *sex*—males are institutionalized with greater frequency than females; *legal status*—

Table 4–3. The DMH Population: Patients' Characteristics as Predictors of Readmission

Predictor Variable	Beta	f	P	R
Age	.200	120.3	.00001	.22
Marital status	-.051	26.5	.00001	.24
Sex	.051	25.9	.00001	.26
Legal status	.049	23.4	.00001	.27
Race (black)	.042	19.0	.00001	.29
Psychodiagnosis (schizo)	.040	13.4	.00002	.30
Tinley	.103	49.3	.00001	.38
Manteno	.087	29.6	.00001	.42
ISPI	.073	23.6	.00001	.45
Read	.064	14.7	.00002	.46

voluntary patients have more episodes of prior admission; *race*—blacks are more likely to have been admitted on repeated occasions; and *psychodiagnosis*—schizophrenic patients appear at psychiatric hospitals more often than any of the other diagnostic groupings. Also, cases treated at *Tinley Park* and *Manteno* are more likely to be chronic patients, while those admitted to *ISPI* and *Read* are less likely to have been hospitalized on multiple prior occasions. The above variables accounted for approximately 21 percent of the variance in the criterion measure.

Thinking Prospectively

If we go beyond the usual retrospective approach to data collection and think prospectively about the issue, that is, ask who readmits to the hospital over the year that we followed our patients, a surprising and important finding appears. If we ask in a given year, "What are the correlates of readmission?" we find the opposite of our retrospective analysis, namely, that the *younger* and the *less severely ill* are more likely to readmit.

Research design plays an essential role in how the issue of readmission is viewed. If we look backward, we see the older, more impaired patient as the recidivist. If we look forward, it is the less severely impaired young patients who are the recidivist group. In other words, the picture changes dramatically.

If we turn our attention to a prospective analysis of the same group, we find a very different picture of readmissions emerging. We interviewed 208 of our sample of 313 state mental patients at least once after their initial hospitalization, usually about six months later. We compiled admissions information on this group over the year following the initial hospitalization and first interview.

The 208 people who comprise this panel were required to have a place to live and some type of steady income before they could be released from the hospital. Almost half (41 percent) were living with another person(s), i.e., a parent, relative, or friend, when they were contacted to be reinterviewed in the community. One-third of the sample (32 percent) were living in intermediate shelter care facilities, nursing homes, or the like. Only about 25 percent were living on their own. Five people (2 percent) were homeless at the time we interviewed them in the community, i.e., they had become undomiciled between their hospital release and the second interview. Almost everyone was receiving some type of public assistance (79 percent) or money from family or friends in order to live. Even people who had jobs before entering the hospital were now receiving public aid. Ninety percent of the sample reported holding a job at one time, but only 16 percent were employed three months before their hospital admission.

About two-thirds (64 percent) of the sample at the time of the second interview were men and over half (55 percent) were black. Whites comprised 36 percent of the sample; Hispanics and other minorities represented another 9 percent. The people in our study were primarily young and uneducated. Over half were under thirty years of age and did not have high school diplomas. Most of the sample were never married, separated, or divorced. Only 6 percent were currently married. Since most of the people were receiving public assistance, the average income per month for our sample was low, just under $400 per month. A few people (10 percent) earned as much as $900 per month, but they earned their income from such illegal activities as dealing drugs, prostitution, or pimping.

Most of the people in our Time 2 sample had many difficulties to overcome. Most of them were poor, black, young, and uneducated.

Add to this the presence of mental illness and we have a sample of people who we would expect to have great difficulty getting along in the community.

Diagnostic Description

At the time of the initial interview in the hospital, about two-thirds of our sample had been hospitalized at least one time before. Almost half were diagnosed as schizophrenic (47 percent) and 42 percent as affective disordered. The other 11 percent were diagnosed with some character disorder. Seventy percent of the blacks and 58 percent of the people of other minorities were diagnosed as schizophrenic, while most of the whites (55 percent) were diagnosed as affective disordered ($\chi^2 = 26.16$; df = 4; p < .05). When they were interviewed in the hospital, half the people in our sample had been there for thirty days or more. When we reinterviewed them in the community, 42 percent had returned to the hospital at least once since the time of their first interview. About half of those who returned to the hospital spent as little as two months in the community.

The hospitalization history of our sample describes a group of people who were hospital-dependent, i.e., most of them had been previously hospitalized and once they were released from the hospital spent little time in the community. Indeed, life for these people was a constant flow of hospitalization, release to the community, and rehospitalization. Since most of the people in the sample lived with someone or in some shelter care facility, these people were cared for by someone else for the better part of their lives, so the decision to rehospitalize them often included other people besides the patient and state hospital personnel.

A regression analysis was performed on the dependent measure of readmissions during the study period, entering the person's name for his/her problem along with the other control variables of sex, race, education, age, hospital diagnosis, and time between interviews. Then variables were introduced into the analysis in terms of their hypothesized causal ordering in the lives of the people in the study. We entered the variables of race and sex and then age and education in the regression analysis. Next we entered diagnosis and

Table 4–4. The MHPP Sample: Variables Affecting Rehospitalization

| | Extent of Attenuation for Measurement Error | | |
| | Unstandardized Regression Coefficients | | |
Variable Name	Uncorrected	Small Correction	Large Correction
Function (T1)	0.00621	−0.01026	−0.01763
Activity (T1)	−0.01464	−0.01470	−0.01567
GAS (T1)	−0.01826*	−0.01941*	−0.01950*
Prev. adm.	0.05269**	0.05464**	0.05322**
Gender	−0.29169	−0.19044	−0.19411
White	−0.12466	−0.04047	−0.07602
Other race	−0.48156	−0.50436	−0.51017
Age	−0.02809**	−0.03155**	−0.02989**
Education	−0.04508	−0.04894	−0.05196
Affective dis.	0.07462	−0.00423	−0.05193
Character dis.	0.71152*	0.89748*	0.92823*
Non-psych. prob.	0.14516	0.13835	−0.05275
External prob.	0.03709	−0.05837	−0.31456
No prob.	−0.24441	−0.55767	−0.94787
Missing prob.	0.02285	−0.02111	−0.30467
Time in study	0.00238	0.00021	0.00021
Constant	2.12814	3.15442	3.49132

**p<.01	F=3.96025**	F=3.83917**	F=3.89356**
*p<.10	df=16	df=16	df=16
	R square=.24911	R square=.24334	R square=.24594

problem name and finally controlled for the time between interviews in examining readmissions.

We ran this analysis three times (table 4–4), once without any correction for measurement error, a second time with a small attenuation for measurement error, and a third time with a large attenuation for measurement error. On average, members of the sample had been readmitted once between interviews. Older people returned less often than younger people, and those diagnosed as character disordered had more admissions than people in other diagnostic categories. As the time between interviews increased, so did the number of times people were readmitted to the hospital.

As we controlled for measurement error in the analyses, the effects of age decreased slightly and the effects of being character disordered increased, while the significance of time between interviews disappeared. Attenuation for measurement error did not affect the overall findings.

Being young and being diagnosed as character disordered is positively related to being rehospitalized in the prospective research design.

A comparison of the two research approaches to the readmissions problem produces an unmistakable result. If one uses the retrospective approach, readmissions looks like a problem of older, severely disturbed patients. But if we analyze the problem prospectively, we get the opposite result, namely, that the younger, less severely disordered patient with a history of previous admissions is the one more likely to be readmitted. Less severe illness and youth are the characteristics of the recidivist. The implications are profound: readmission is a problem of the young, less severely impaired. What brings this group back to the hospital?

We begin with a few of the reasons patients give for returning to the hospital, and then we more systematically describe the road back to the hospital in the next chapter.

I was sleeping in the hallway. The police got a call from a lady in my cousin's building. They told me to get out of the hallway and go down the street. I told them it was public property, and why should I? They took me to jail. They issued an order of detention to come here. I told them I was King James and they couldn't understand that. I told them they weren't my doctor and they didn't have the right to send me here.

* * *

I had been here three weeks before. I had met a girl here and we got really tight. We talked about everything. We were going to get an apartment and take care of her baby together. But when we got out everything had changed. She acted like a different person. She'd talk down to me like I was a kid. She put her baby up for adoption. When I got out last time there'd been an outstanding warrant for my arrest, so I spent two weeks in jail. When I got out, she was a different personality. People had warned me, but I didn't see that side of her 'til it was too late. I was depressed and feeling like killing myself, so I came here. I walked.

* * *

My brother-in-law came over to watch me because they thought I was acting crazy. We were in front of a beef stand and he had ahold of my arm. I told him to let go of my arm or I would throw Coke in his face. He didn't, so I did. He beat the shit out of me in front of that beef stand. I ran home and told my mother to call the police. But instead of doing that they called the police and had them bring me here to the nuthouse.

I had been acting a little strange because of my manic thing. But I could've gotten some other help besides coming here. This is a terrible place. My brother-in-law is very jealous of me. He has propositioned me before. I thought when the police came that they were going to trick Ricky [brother-in-law] into going with them. Instead, I was the one who got tricked. I went crazy in the paddy wagon. I started fantasizing that they were tricking me to get married and other bizarre things.

* * *

My sister brought me in. I couldn't sleep. I thought the baby's head fell off, and I was trying to get it back on. [There was no baby. Interviewer.] Voices were coming through the wall. I didn't sleep for three nights. Her and my daughter took turns staying up. I was nervous and shaky. When I laid down somebody said: I'm going to kill you. I was afraid. I was going from room to room all the time. I knew I needed some kind of help.

In all of these examples, either the individual or those around him recognized that something was wrong and that this situation was sufficiently unpleasant or irritating to warrant action of a remedial kind.

In each instance, the more familiar manifestations of psycho-pathological disorder—hallucinations, delusions, life-threatening mood swings—were embedded in a rich and dynamic interactive setting. Usually, a variety of people in the individual's environment—family members, friends, fellow patients, physicians, mental health professionals, law enforcement officials, neighbors, strangers—were in one way or another involved with his or her troubles.

We have argued that the state hospital has been transformed but has not lost its central role in the treatment of the poor mentally ill. If the goal of the state system is to release the patient to civil society, then those who are in need of what the state hospital offers will find themselves returning regularly when the need arises. Entry into the state hospital is a function of important social and economic factors in association with clinical issues, and reentry is more a function of the choices of both the patients and those who must cope with them over time when conflicts arise.

In the next chapter, we take a closer look at the patients from our sample who went back to the hospital. We know from chapter 3 that there is not much help for patients outside the hospital. In chapter 5, we see how that fact plays out in the lives of the troubled and troublesome patients who return to the hospital.

PATHS BACK TO THE HOSPITAL

In this chapter we take a close look at patients who are readmitted to the state hospital and the different paths that lead them back. We have seen through our prospective analysis that the younger, less severely impaired patients with a history of previous admissions are the most likely group to return. But if we are to reduce the number of readmissions we must look more carefully at this group in order to understand the factors that led to their return to the state hospital. To do that, we identified a subgroup of patients who were readmitted during the course of the research project. This subsample of readmittees was drawn from among the patients in the total sample of 313 who returned to the hospital between the first and second interviews (roughly a six-month interval). We interviewed the patient, the clinician involved in the readmission, and the person who brought the patient to the hospital in order to get a clearer picture of the readmissions process.

The method for selecting informants was as follows. In a ten-week period from March through May 1986, those informants from the total sample who were readmitted to two of the four Chicago state mental hospitals were approached by an interviewer. The two hospitals were Chicago-Read Mental Health Center and Madden Mental Health Center.

During the interview period, the medical records office at Madden and Read contacted the interviewers as soon as a patient of the total sample was admitted. During the interview period, thirty-six patients from that sample were readmitted in the two target hospitals; seventeen of these were interviewed for the present study. Of the other nineteen patients, nine were discharged, four were transferred to one of the nontarget hospitals, three went on unauthorized leave of absence before they could be approached, one patient was deflected, and two patients were approached, but refused to participate. In table 5–1, the readmission sample is compared to (1) the sample of 313 patients initially studied and (2) a population of 10,068 separate

Table 5–1. Readmitted Patients: Demographic Composition

	Readmission Sample (N=17)	MHPP Sample (N=313)	DMH Population (N=10,068)
Sex			
Male	76.5%	63.3%	60.7%
Female	23.5	36.7	39.3
Race			
Black	58.8	55.3	58.9
White	41.2	34.8	33.1
Other	—	10.0	5.0
Age			
18–34	58.8	66.7	61.4
35–49	35.3	23.0	26.6
50–65	5.9	10.2	12.0

admissions to the Chicago-area state hospitals in the period July 1, 1983–December 31, 1984.

We show in this chapter that there are three kinds of trouble that lead someone back to the hospital. Each involves an intricate interplay among symptoms, personal conflict, and service options. We begin with a discussion of personal trouble, which involves the patient's attempt to handle his troubles himself, and then discuss how family and service options create situations in which the state hospital becomes the best way to resolve the problems at hand.

Personal Trouble

Fred, while in a good mood one day, bought a bottle of cheap port on the way home, and went back to his hotel room and drank it all. Under the influence of the alcohol, he experienced a surge of guilt and anxiety: "I don't really know everything that happened. All I know was that I was really boozed up. I guess I was hearing voices. I might have killed myself. There was really nobody there to help me you know. . . . I started getting suicidal feelings, paranoid feelings, like people were talking about me."

Many readmittees, like Fred, experienced overwhelming feelings after the use of alcohol. Alcohol consumption is involved in many readmissions. Michael provides another example. After he had consumed a six-pack of beer at a party, he couldn't sleep that night and started to hear voices again. Eric had alcohol problems too. When after a night of drinking he checked himself into the emergency room of a general hospital because he felt "overwhelmed, distraught, depressed a bit," he recognized that the alcohol intensified his negative feelings: "When you're drinking, the thought that nobody cares about me increases tenfold."

Wayne's readmission was also preceded by overwhelming and intolerable feelings, but in his case they consisted mostly of anger and depression. He explained that he decided to have himself admitted again because he felt that he "got sick":

What do you mean when you say that you got sick? I wasn't eating right. Eating became a burden. I had no interest in eating. I was going to bed at 6:30 at night, sleeping. That's when I know that I'm getting sick again, when I go to bed early. I felt terrible. I wasn't talking to no one. I'd sit there by myself and I didn't want to have nothing to do with no one. . . .

How severe is your problem? You mean depression? Oh, terrible. You can't function properly. At 4 in the afternoon I'm emotionally drained from sitting around thinking.

All of these men experienced strong and often intensely painful negative feelings, but what turned their experience into trouble, that is, into the kind of problem that could not be left unattended and required immediate attention, is that all of them felt that they could no longer control their feelings and, by implication, their actions. Fred, for example, expressed this clearly when he said:

I don't know how to handle myself when I get this way. Not fight but out of control. I don't know how to pull myself together. You might call that embarrassing. I get that way quite often. . . . I'm scared of myself. Not so much that I will fight or get violent. I just need some help. I don't know how to handle myself.

What do you fear most about your problem? I don't know how to control it. That's what scares me. . . . It changes my whole personality you might say, and then it leaves me frightened.

Eric observed that the effects of excessive alcohol intake contributed to this experience of having no control over the intensity of one's feelings: "I really do not make a scene in public. When I'm depressed I get so overwhelmed I just leave. Only when I'm drunk. I mean, I have bad feelings when I'm sober but I'm in control of them."

As Fred indicated, the sensation of having no control over his emotions, of being swept away in a maelstrom of distressing feelings, was acutely frightening. In some men, this took the form of a fear that they would impulsively commit suicide. Fred, as we have seen, reported that he feared that he might kill himself, and Wayne, when asked what he feared most about his depression, answered, "I think eventually I will commit suicide."

These men became emotionally distraught and acutely suicidal. They returned to the mental hospital on their own initiative. Let us take a closer look at Wayne's situation, for example. Wayne's account of his depression is embedded in a long list of worries, complaints, and grievances. His main grievance is the halfway house. When asked who suggested that he go to the hospital for help, he answered: "No one. I came myself. I tell you, I've seen a lot of sick people that sit around talking to themselves, hearing voices. And Clayton lets them sit around for two weeks without sending them to the hospital. I said to myself: You belong in the hospital. Why don't they bring you in? So when I got sick Tuesday morning I said to myself: I'm gonna go to the hospital. I'm not even going to ask these people."

But it was not only his conviction that he was neglected that angered Wayne; he also objected to the many institutional rules and routines that governed life in the halfway house. For example:

Did you have problems with the rules at the facility? Yeah. You can't stay in your room. Every time you go out you got to sign out. . . . I know what the future was at the Clayton. I couldn't smoke, I couldn't drink. . . . Where's the freedom here?

Often, Wayne directed considerable anger at seemingly minor issues: "I didn't have the caffeine in the morning. They had me on Advil to sleep. But I'm so used to living on my own and drink coffee and have a cigarette in the morning. But they have decaf here. I wouldn't wake up. I would just sit there."

Wayne did not like that the halfway house acted as the recipient of his SSDI allowance to pay for board and care and granted him a monthly allowance of $25. Other grievances in Wayne's life concerned work and family. Being unemployed was particularly hard on his self-esteem, and with regard to his family, he felt abandoned by his children and was convinced that his brother and his brother's girlfriend had cheated him out of money:

Did you have family problems? I already told you. My brother sold the car and didn't give me the money. And I needed the money for clothes and other things. And like I said, with this girlfriend all the time. Taking my checks when I'm in the hospital. I could've bought clothes for them. Now I'm down to what I wear. It's not good. Especially when you're sick. They're all ganging up on you.

Wayne appeared in the interview as a lonesome, suspicious, and deeply isolated man. Several times during the interview he seemed to acknowledge this, for example when he said: "When I'm by myself, I like it so much that when I'm with other people I get, not nervous, but I don't get along so well with everybody else. I don't get involved in conversations." Wayne's story echoes many themes— isolation, a sense of powerlessness, the dominating presence of paternalistic, bureaucratic rules, unemployment, poverty, abandonment by family, loss of self-esteem—that are common in the lives of readmittees. The mundane worries about coffee, cigarettes, unemployment, and isolation combine into a meaningful world of fears and problems.

Family Trouble

Not every readmission took place on the initiative of an individual who experienced overwhelming distress. In fact, most of the individuals in our sample returned to the hospital because someone wanted them hospitalized. In most of these cases, the patient had caused trouble for the family, and they felt his behavior could no longer be tolerated.

Let us look at some of the ways in which recidivist patients get in trouble. Some people irritate those close to them by their seemingly irrational behavior. Dorothy exasperated her employer by what looked like her unwillingness to take care of herself. He gave several examples of her refusal to provide him with her date of birth, to sign a tax return that he prepared for her, or to wear a set of reading glasses that he had ordered for her. As he concluded: "The only thing that I be scared about was a total lack of self-direction. There was absolutely nothing that she would do for herself. She was not crazy. No, I don't think she is crazy. Very slow, yes."

Some of the patients in our sample taxed their companions with their self-destructive behavior. Lewis's family had given up on him because of his heroin addiction. On the day of his readmission, he had cashed his welfare check, spent the larger part of it on the repayment of some debts, and from the remaining money bought heroin. Intoxicated by heroin and alcohol, he presented himself at his sister's house, where, according to hospital records, he was "verbally and physically abusive, and confronted other people with irrelevant observations." Subsequent attempts by the hospital staff to involve the sister in Lewis's treatment failed. According to Lewis's treatment coordinator the sister "didn't want to have anything to do with him. She was not so controlled when I spoke to her on the phone. In a hostile tone she said: He ain't coming here."

Both Lewis and Dorothy displayed bizarre and unusual behavior. But, although persons around them considered their behavior puzzling or troublesome, the unusualness by itself was not considered a threat and was therefore insufficient reason to spur the readmission.

For families to act upon a member's behavior by starting admission procedures requires more than just the bizarre behavior. When the member's behavior is interpreted as posing a serious threat to the family's standing in the community or when the member's behavior is grossly indecent or threatening to his or her own safety, swift and decisive remedial action is undertaken.

In the most common example, a family is spurred to contain the behavior of one of its members when that member resorts to actual violence. The fear of bodily harm or worse, the constantly recurring turmoil, and in particular, the unmanageability of the individual's behavior quite literally make life impossible for the family. Most relatives of a formerly hospitalized patient who was prone to violent behavior stressed the almost unendurable nature of the situation. As Renee's mother, in discussing her daughter's violence toward the family, expressed it, "It was a living hell."

Most readmittees who were violent also displayed other problems, such as exaggerated suspicion, confusion, or hearing voices. Yet, as the following quote from Jack's mother shows, the repeated violent behavior of the patient is the strongest stimulus for members of the family to readmit: "It turns out. . . . At that time I was talking to Jack's doctor. I was worried about his hearing voices and his paranoia. He said he was being followed all the time. Jack's doctor thought it was a good idea that he would be admitted to Read. We were all physically afraid of Jack. If you have witnessed his rages, you would have been afraid too." Initially, Jack's mother places the admission in the context of his alleged delusions and auditory hallucinations, but then, as if to provide a definitive justification for the suggestion to admit Jack to a mental hospital, she discloses the family's fear of his violence.

Although the violent aspects of the individual's behavior tended to dominate the family's experience, other aspects were an integral part of the family's understanding of that trouble. For example, Jack's diabetes, the sense of being different that this instilled in him, and the resulting anger and hostility were all part of an explanatory scheme that his mother employed to understand Jack's behavior. Jack's mother perceived his diabetes as the cause of his trouble and sought to address this problem by arranging for adequate medical care. Renee's parents framed their daughter's violence in terms of a developmental disorder and sought help in the form of special schools and behavioral programs. Ralph's parents understood their son's violent behavior as drug-induced and accordingly tried to place him in a drug treatment program.

Personal and family trouble illustrate the two kinds of trouble that lead back to the hospital. In the first instance, the individual evaluates his own situation and acts; in the second instance, the individual is evaluated and acted upon by others. In the second case, the nature of the trouble is strongly dependent on the framework that others bring to the particular situation. An example is a readmission that is the result not of actual violence, but of the threat of violence as perceived by others. This was particularly true when earlier admissions to the mental hospital had been accompanied by violence on the part of the patient. Behavior that appeared rather innocent and inconspicuous quickly took on an ominous meaning as the first sign of a recurrence of violent behavior. The following description of the onset of a manic episode in Paul, which would eventually result in his readmission, illustrates this process of anxiously reading the recidivist's behavior. The story is told by Larry, a public service attorney and close friend of Paul, who was instrumental in having him readmitted to the hospital: "I was fully aware of his prior hospitalizations. He phoned me and said that he wanted to get together for coffee. I said: Come on over. Come the next day. He phoned in the evening. He has done that before. To come to see me before he gets sick. I didn't notice it then. I didn't notice it this time."

Paul comes over to Larry's house, where the two of them discuss Paul's therapy at an experimental program for psycho-affective disorders. Larry continues:

When he left he said: Come on over to my house sometime and look at my new paintings. A few days later he phoned and said, this was on a Saturday: Let's have coffee tomorrow morning. I said: Yes. He said: Let's do it at your house. So I said fine, but I began to worry. It was different from the original plan to see his paintings. That phone call, by the way, was at 6:45 in the morning. Five minutes later he phoned again. He said: Carol Morse just called. She's got a big job for me to do, so I'll see you at the end of the week, and give my love to your fish. He hung up. At this point I knew he was going downhill fast.

What made you think that he was going downhill? Something in the tone of his voice. He sounded manicky, even angry. Plus, saying, "Give my love to your fish," for Paul, is totally off the wall.

Then I learned that he'd shown up to work drunk. He makes a living by doing carpeting, odd jobs. In premorbid days Paul was not a drinker. Occasionally a glass of whiskey or a glass of wine. He smoked a lot of marijuana, but he was not a drinker. Immediately prior to his being incarcerated in jail in Mexico, which was his first psychotic episode, now seven or eight years ago, he had consumed a lot of tequila. . . . Once he got out of that hospital he would never drink because of his medication. Except prior to his hospitalizations he would drink a lot. Also one day he showed up to work with purple eyebrows. I know when he's sick he gets preoccupied with sex. He sees himself as a superstud. He has been violent in bed with his girlfriend.

The behavior suggests a familiar pattern to the observer. The gravity of the situation derives from the memory of earlier instances of the patient's violence, which translates into an expectation that he might resort to violence again. As the following quote by Larry shows, it is this repeated referral to earlier instances of violence that guides the observer's assessment of the situation:

> Then, a Friday night, and Paul's brother Bill calls me from Phoenix to say that he had spoken to Paul on the phone and so had their parents, and they knew that he was sick again. On two prior occasions Bill had been up here and instrumental in getting Paul hospitalized. . . . Then he asked me to do something about it. . . . Bill laid a guilt trip on me. Saying: Paul gets drunk and gets into fights in bars. Smashes his car. Starts ritual fires in his house which sometimes leads to burning of furniture. I got mad. I said: I know these problems. We'll do something about it.

Larry's story is instructive. It usually takes an accumulation of behavioral indicators, all pointing in the same direction, plus some form of corroboration of the initial suspicions (by actual violence, or, as in this case, by similar assessments by others) to initiate remedial action.

Institutional Trouble

Many readmittees resided in one of the community facilities that provide care and supervision to mental patients. These halfway houses, nursing homes, group homes, and board-and-care facilities supplement the function of the state hospital. Their role in the spectrum of mental health services goes beyond the mere provision of residence to formerly hospitalized mental patients in that they also provide supervision and/or treatment and are usually paid by a third party.

As we will see, community institutional facilities play an important, and so far not very well understood, role in the readmission of formerly hospitalized mental patients. We introduce our analysis by returning once more to Dorothy.

After she had to leave her employer and before she was readmitted, Dorothy spent some time in an emergency shelter. The shelter is intended for people who find themselves in a temporary housing crisis. It usually does not accept people with a history of admissions to a mental hospital. Clients are accepted on condition that they find a job within a period of two weeks, and to that end, they are required to make three job applications a day. Each resident in fact signs an agreement to this condition upon admission to the facility. Dorothy, whose history of mental hospitalization was known to the shelter staff, was considered an inappropriate client

> because of the mental illness. She couldn't communicate. She couldn't look for work. She did try. What she did was stopping people on the street and asking them if they needed a house-keeper. She would go on about the Princess of Trinidad. When you talked to her and asked her a straight question she would say: I'm the Princess of Trinidad. We're not qualified to deal with mental illness. Also, people have to make three formal work calls a day. And we call and check on them. If they don't they get a formal warning and they're only allowed three formal warnings.

> *What happens after that?* We usually throw them out. But 95 percent are usually appropriate. . . .

Dorothy was unable or unwilling to abide by the basic rule that residents actively work toward a resumption of their independence. She was regarded by the shelter staff as a difficult case. To the shelter, Dorothy constituted a management problem, a threat to the shelter's organizational integrity. As the counselor explained, "Dorothy was a hard one. We tried to have her into work, a live-in housekeeper somewhere. She wouldn't do it. She kept thinking her main purpose was to clean here. We tried to encourage her to become independent. . . . She tried so hard to please everybody, but she couldn't do what we wanted her to do, so she failed here."

Dorothy presented the organization with some real problems. Some of her behavior was bizarre, incomprehensible, and irritating. On various occasions she would refer to herself as the "Virgin of Chicago" or the "Immaculate Conception," and she was reported at times to ignore salutations and to scrub arduously the shelter's floor each day, despite the activity of a professional cleaning service. However, a counselor, reflecting on the readmission, expressed surprise at the fact that Dorothy was admitted to the hospital, because: "Dorothy . . . was not a threat. In fact she was not even that bizarre, except for every once in a while. And all the residents liked her."

As the counselor explained, very few options to transfer Dorothy were available to the shelter. She was turned down by another shelter in one of the suburbs, and the shelters in Chicago were considered too violent and dangerous for her. The only remaining alternative was to refer her to a nearby psychiatric crisis center. This made it necessary to present Dorothy as someone in an acute psychiatric crisis, who badly needed a psycho-diagnostic assessment. This is exactly how Dorothy was perceived by the staff psychiatrist at the crisis center. As he described her: "She was confused and delusional. She came to us from a shelter where they noticed that she had been very confused. They could not handle her, so they sent her here."

Jack was readmitted from a nursing home after he had verbally threatened the staff and, in a rage, threatened to kill himself. As he commented after his arrival in the hospital: "They [the nursing home staff] told me I couldn't go back. When you say you're going committing suicide, they take it seriously. You can't kid around with that. When you say it here [in the mental hospital] they laugh you know."

Institutional trouble in community facilities often originates in rule violation. The individual's continued presence in such surroundings depends on following the rules. The rules that govern behavior of the users of such institutions tend to be simple and intrusive. The rules and the standards for assessing their applications are stated in clear, unambiguous terms: "Smoke only in designated smoking areas"; "Have sleeping area tidy daily by 10:00 a.m." Usually the standards that govern rule application are stated in simple terms, so that residents' behavior can be neatly divided into two nonoverlapping categories of "in accordance with" and "in violation of" the rules.

Community facilities' explicit rules extend to many areas of life that in more private circumstances would be considered the province of an individual's own judgment and discretion. Most residential facilities have rules concerning exit from and entry to the facility, access to the living quarters of other residents, a curfew, amount of money allotted for individual spending, sexual conduct, consumption of alcohol, opportunity and location for cigarette smoking, and the like. In some instances, when the individual is part of a behavior modification program, rules are formulated in meticulous detail about how to behave in various situations and what sanctions are imposed upon the individual who deviates from the rules.

Even the simplest and most mundane of organizational tasks,

such as the timely dispensing of meals, requires coordination of the behavior of residents and staff members. Many rules pertain to licensing criteria or safety standards. For example, the rules, much maligned by residents, that govern smoking are a direct product of fire regulations. To the resident who spends most of his day with little else to do but socialize in the day room of the facility, restrictions on smoking or on the extent of one's relation to other residents are easily experienced as unnecessary intrusions.

When we asked Pearl, Fred's friend, why, in her opinion, Fred had to return to the hospital, she gave the following answer: "I think it was the medicine he was taking that made him do that. It used to work on him in a funny way. He gets disturbed . . . not disturbed, but melancholy. Then the first thing he thinks of is the hospital, you know. . . . I guess he gets melancholy and he says: I go to the hospital. They always helped him."

Patient Preferences

A readmission occurs in the historical context of earlier admissions—in Fred's case, forty-three of them. Fred's former admissions comprise a large reservoir of personal experience that inevitably influences his present attitude toward the mental hospital. To Fred, the hospital had come to mean support to such an extent that to a man in Fred's circumstances it becomes the first thing to think of in times of trouble.

Readmitted patients are familiar with the mental hospital and the intricate network of social services in which it is embedded. Many of them, for example, had spent time in different hospitals and, as a result, had outspoken opinions about the differences between hospitals in quality of care, hygiene, or the ease with which prerogatives such as a grounds pass could be obtained. Jessie expressed this when she said: "Some hospitals are O.K., some are not. Saint Anne's was O.K. That was the best hospital I've ever been in."

And Ralph's mother explicitly prefers Madden Mental Health Center over Tinley Park because the first, in her opinion, "has a better program."

Not only are some hospitals preferred over others, but in some instances the mental hospital is preferred to other service modalities. For example, on many occasions the hospital staff has suggested that, given the need for a close monitoring of his physical ailments, Clarence should be referred to a nursing home. Clarence's sister, however, vehemently opposed this suggestion and considered Madden Mental Health Center the ideal solution to her brother's problems: "The doctor asked me do I wanna put him in a home. I said: Hell, no! When he's sick I make sure he gets to the doctor in the hospital. 'Cause that's what the hospital is for: sick people."

And Fred makes it clear that he prefers professional help over the attention of friends or fellow residents when he suffers from mood swings: "I don't talk to people in the hotel, because I don't want them to know my history. I don't even go to the landlady downstairs. I rather don't tell it to strangers. I just want professional help."

Not surprisingly, many of our informants were quite particular about the hospital they wanted to be admitted to. They did not choose a mental hospital in general, but were specific about the particular hospital, and sometimes even the particular ward they preferred. Jack, for example, after he decided that he wanted to return to the hospital, called up his old ward: "I was up all night. I came here in the morning. I called up Read first, the C-South unit, to see if there was room. Sometimes they let you wait for three or four hours. But they said: Sure Jack, come on by. . . . They're friends here. They have a drinking problem."

Lewis specifically asked the police to bring him to Madden Mental Health Center. Frank illustrates the strength of our informants' preferences and the persistence with which they pursue them when he went on unauthorized leave of absence while at Madden upon hearing he was about to be transferred to Chicago-Read: "I escaped from Madden last time because they wanted to send me to Read. Read is a real hell-hole. People there urinate on themselves, waste on themselves, and nobody cares. There are roaches all over the place."

To attain their goal of gaining entrance to a preferred hospital, many readmittees use their extensive knowledge of the system, acquired through years of experience. Many of them knew, for example, the exact boundaries of a hospital's catchment area. They were familiar with the overt and hidden criteria for admission, the intricacies of commitment procedures, the advantages of a voluntary over an involuntary admission, the number of days one could be admitted without losing one's SSI eligibility, and so on. Some adjusted their address to fit the catchment area of the preferred hospital. Ralph's mother describes how, to gain him entrance to Madden, she asserted in the intake office that her son no longer lived with the family but with his uncle on the West Side: "After we got to Madden, Ralph had to sign himself in. I knew if I would give my own address they would bring him to Tinley Park. So I told them he didn't live with us at all. I thought Madden had a better program."

Another common strategy is based on the individual's knowledge of what constitutes compelling criteria for admission. Hospital admission criteria are derived from the legal standard for civil commitment as formulated in the state's commitment statute. The legal grounds for application for admission have resulted in two practical criteria for voluntary admission: dangerousness to self or others, as expressed, for example, in threats of suicide or homicide; and the inability to take care of self as a result of gross impairment of thought, mood, perception, or judgment.

Symptom Management and Readmission

Most of the readmittees were well aware of these criteria and the way they functioned in the admission procedure. They knew very well, for example, that in case of doubt, because of the legal/administrative context of the admission procedure and its attendant risks, the intake worker would err on the side of admitting. Patients and their families had no reservations in using this knowledge to their advantage.

The most straightforward way of applying this knowledge about admission criteria and procedures is simply to report, upon request, the necessary psychopathological qualifications. Given impending suicide or the presence of hallucinations, the clinician has little recourse to independent behavioral criteria to substantiate the patient's assertions and has to rely primarily on what the patient tells him. Several of our informants reported gaining admission by using this form of symptom simulation. Chip, for example, recounted:

I signed myself in, voluntarily. They didn't want me to come in because they thought there was nothing wrong with me. But I convinced them that I had no place to stay.

How did you do that? They asked me if I was hearing voices and I said yes. [Laughs] It's not hard to act crazy with all the experience I have. . . .

Frank gained entrance by stating that he intended to kill himself: "I came here, and I knew that if I told them I was a junkie they wouldn't let me in, so I told them I was suicidal. They would have told me to get on a methadone program."

In these examples, the patient used his working knowledge of the admission procedure to structure the interaction with the intake worker in such a way that admission was inevitable. The patient, by summoning the realities of the hospital's legal/administrative environment, effectively restrained the intake worker from acting on any suspicions the latter might have about the patient's real intentions. The intake worker had no choice but to admit, even if each party was aware of the other's hidden agenda. The following statement from Fred's intake worker at the emergency room illustrates the complex shadow play that goes on between patient and provider during admission.

> *Did you consider sending Fred home?* Yes, we talked about that. I will always ask about possible support systems. He said he had no one. I asked about professionals. He said: I can't get ahold of her. Then I asked the usual question: What would happen, Fred, if we sent you home today? He said: I'd take the pills. That puts us in the ethical and legal position to certify him. We had no choice. He had given us no choice. He was pleased obviously, because he wanted to be in the hospital. I know I have no choice but to get him in a safe environment for the night. I don't feel he fakes it. He feels worthless or hopeless. I don't know if he would take the pills, but we can't gamble on it.

In most of these examples, the individual resorted to outright deceit to gain readmission. As Fred's case illustrates, however, in certain cases the manipulation of admission criteria took a less blunt and—with respect to the readmission process—probably much more important and ubiquitous form. Despite her awareness of Fred's manipulation, his intake worker was convinced that he did not fake his problems.

According to the medical records, Rosa was admitted after "she created a disturbance at a Walgreen drugstore," where allegedly she had drawn the attention of the sales staff by "acting in a confused manner." Upon admission, she was still found to be "very confused," with "severe impairment of cognitive functions." In addition, "the associations were loose" and the "judgment severely impaired."

We asked Rosa about the circumstances of her readmission, and she did not deny that the police took her from a public place—according to Rosa it was a Burger King restaurant—but asserted that she was admitted because she herself decided to return to the hospital. As she said: "I needed help, and I thought this [Chicago-Read] was the place to come for help, since I've been here through my sickness. I needed help to find me a place to live."

These different perspectives on Rosa's admission present us with a perplexing issue. How do we explain the divergence between the hospital's version of Rosa's hospitalization and her own account? Does Rosa's account represent a denial of her mental disorder, or is she an exceptionally talented actress who, by feigning psychiatric symptoms, obtains admission to the mental hospital?

Rosa's treatment coordinator struggled with the same vexing questions. At first he described his patient as "extremely delusional. That's why we accepted her. She has very poor judgment. She doesn't have a place to live." But, he then continued with: "I talked with the patient about why she needed to be readmitted. She told me point-blank that she had no place to live. She told me she went from shelter to shelter. She was walking down the street. The police picked her up and brought her there. She denied she acted bizarre for the police to pick her up. I have a feeling she acted such that she knew she would be picked up." However, when we asked him if Rosa was behaving in ways that were unusual or embarrassing, he answered: "My strong feeling is she was. She won't admit it." Finally, when asked about the cause of Rosa's repeated admissions, he answered: "My feeling is that it is because she has no stable place to live. Secondly, she does present multiple delusions. While the delusions are not encapsuled, she only uses them for her own benefit. She doesn't get in trouble without her wanting to get in trouble."

As we remember, Fred's readmission was inaugurated by an onslaught of overwhelming feelings of loneliness and anxiety after he drank a bottle of port wine. Fred gave the following description of the events:

I stopped, on the way back to my place, around 4–4:40 p.m., in that grocery store and bought me a bottle of dark port. That is cheap wine, you know. I kept forgetting if I took my medication and I took five or six of them. And I got suicidal; strung out and suicidal.

In my apartment I drank the bottle, with ice and a glass. I could kill myself, you know. To drink that whole bottle. Jesus! And it's wine. It's not beer, you know. It makes you sick. It took me about an hour and a half to finish that bottle. . . . I don't really know everything that happened. All I know was that I was really boozed up. I guess I was hearing voices. I might have killed myself. There was nobody there to help me, you know. If I called the psychiatrist at Ravenswood I must have known something was wrong.

As we have seen before, for reasons of his own, Fred's purported goal was to be admitted either to the psychiatric ward of the hospital or to the mental hospital. Fred's presentation was carefully organized to attain this end. As the crisis worker at the emergency room recounted:

He came in on his own. He signed in in the ER. He said he was depressed, he wanted to kill himself and needed to be in the hospital. He has been to our ER many times. . . . He seemed sad. He said he was depressed. He was tearful. When I met him in the ER he had a bag of pills in his hand. He handed them over to me and said: Here, take them or I swallow them all.

Did he recognize you? He seemed to. He said: Hi! He certainly is familiar with the crisis staff. He knows the routine. . . . I sat down with him and said: Fred, what can I help you with? He said: I just can't cope any more. I can't take it. He said he hasn't been eating for days, that he was feeling sad and crying, and that he doesn't know why he is feeling sad and crying. He said that he was taking his meds, but that he was feeling lonely and worthless. . . . Because Fred is a consistent user of our services and his presenting problems are similar, there is no need each time to get a detailed or in-depth interview. He comes in six times a year. That's not a lot really. So this time he presented all the right stuff: I feel hopeless, I feel depressed, I want to kill myself, the voices. And he has the means with his pills. Therefore he is a candidate for hospitalization. . . .

Darell, in an explosion of uncontrolled anger and frustration, assaulted his mother. The attack took place when nobody was home but he and his mother. The mother's detailed description of Darell's behavior during the incident included such details as "he made a real funny noise," "he was kind of foaming at the mouth and breathing heavily." After the attack, neighbors called the police. The police arrived when Darell was home alone; the mother had been taken to the emergency room by the neighbors. The police decided not to intervene and left again. We do not know what transpired between Darell and the police, but he must have presented some modicum of normal behavior, some appearance of not being a security risk, for the police to leave him alone.

After Darell reported being attacked by his brother that same evening, the police returned, and he was finally taken into custody. The police brought him to a mental health center, where he underwent a psychiatric evaluation. The clinical worker gave the following impression:

> He seemed in this deep depression. He didn't seem communicative. I remember that. He seemed to regret the incident, but he seemed overwhelmed by the pressure inside him. . . .

> *Can you tell me more about that pressure?* He was really vague about it. He wasn't talkative about it. He talked in fragments. He was almost tearful.

Finally, that night, Darell was escorted to the mental hospital. On the Intake Evaluation sheet in his medical records, his behavior at intake was described as: ". . . alert, suspicious, denies any medical problems, smiles inappropriately . . . claims to have a lot of things on his mind, but unable to elaborate, very vague. "I just snap." Speech—low monotonous voice, somewhat loose at time, poor concentration . . . affect flat, unable to give exact date. . . ."

Darell presented decidedly different behavior in different circumstances. Toward his mother, to whom he bore a grudge, he acted violent, uncontrolled; toward the police officer who was called to the scene, he was more guarded; and toward the social worker and the intake worker—whom he probably resented but, as he perceived correctly, against whom he was powerless—he was sullen. Darell's behavior was appropriate in each situation.

Paul's friend Larry, on the other hand, noticed a continuity between Paul's psychotic and pre-psychotic behavior:

> Every time he gets out of the hospital he has fewer friends and less devoted family than before. People who know him perceive when he's sick that it's willful. I include myself.

What makes you think that? Even before his first psychotic break he was fiercely independent, judgmental, sure that he was right, kind and loving with an edge of bitterness to it, critical of the world, which is part of being an artist. I think when he gets sick, all that just gets worse, to the point where he goes beyond disagreeing with people, beyond eccentricity, idiosyncrasy.

In those cases in which the individual considers the mental hospital a good solution to his troubles, his desire to enter the hospital influences the expression of his symptoms. He will present himself in a way that enables him to be admitted.

A readmission, given this analysis, is not a mistake or a failure. A readmission is a solution to a real problem. These problems are faced by the patient, his or her family, and the agencies charged with the patient's care. The solution, a readmission, follows from the options one perceives and the difficulties one is facing. The state hospital is the place to take someone who is mentally ill and needs help. There are few alternatives for people with little money. Agencies that are responsible for the care of the mentally ill person choose whom they serve. The problems the mentally ill and their families face are serious. Private agencies who serve state patients need the hospitals as a last resort when problems arise.

This detailed discussion of the factors associated with readmissions has several important implications. Coupled with our statistical analysis of the whole sample, it suggests that interpersonal conflict and the consequent problem solving that most patients, their families, and key service providers do, lead to the readmission. The key question for all involved is, What can be done when trouble arises around the patient? What are the options when he or she does not follow the rules, is in distress, or has emotional, economic, or social problems? The answer for many has been and remains the state hospital. If this conclusion is correct—and the numerous readmissions and the stories told in this chapter seem to bear that out—then community treatment is not really an alternative to the hospital. It is a supplement.

Another equally intriguing implication of this chapter is the effect of all the interpersonal conflict on the criminal justice system. Most of the readmissions we have discussed are triggered by incidents of threatening and rule-violating behavior that can lead to police involvement. What are the problems of criminality that we find among state mental patients? Are the patients with serious criminal histories the same people who are readmitted? We pursue these questions in chapter 8.

Finally, and perhaps most importantly, we see from this chapter that the patients themselves play an important role in the readmission process. They are not passive objects, victims of their disease or some labeling process; rather, they are active participants in the decisions that affect their lives. What they want and think has a strong influence on both the readmissions process and other important policy issues. We develop this theme in the next chapter and show how the patients' definitions of their mental illness affect their overall mental health and ability to function in the community.

HOW PATIENTS GET ALONG IN THE COMMUNITY:
PROBLEM IDENTIFICATION AND MENTAL HEALTH

The last chapter described the lives of readmitting state mental patients and their responses to the problems of being mentally ill and poor. It is a story of conflict and pain, in which the problems of the patients and their families are evident. If we have been successful in depicting the problems of the mentally ill, the reader should now be able to see that the patient plays a vital role in his or her movement through the mental health system. The perceptions, interests, and values of the patient interact with those of others to determine where the patient will live, how he or she will get along with others, and what the course of treatment will be. Of course, family, friends, and professionals also have much to say about the course of events in the patient's life, but the days of thinking that the patient is merely the passive receptacle for a disease process or the labels of others should be put to rest. What the patient wants and how he or she treats others tell a great deal about where that patient lives, how he or she feels, and the kind of treatment received.

In this chapter we move from our discussion of the patient's experiences of the inclusionary system to a more complete discussion of the consequences of this new system for the society at large. To do this, we must return to the larger random sample of state mental patients. Here, we see the variations in patient behavior that follow from the inclusionary policy environment we have created.

First, we need to know how patients function in the community. There are some who think the community is a terrible place for the mentally ill and that they deteriorate outside of institutions. There are others who feel that patients improve in the community as they distance themselves from the debilitating effects of those institutions. Clearly, one of the most important criteria for assessing the
inclusionary system is how it affects the lives of those it purports

to help: improvements in patients' functioning (both clinical and behavioral) are what we expect of human service agencies. There is no better criterion for assessing that functioning than to compare how the same patients fared in the state hospital and in the community.

The next issue we discuss is the impact of the state mental patients on the community: in particular, what threats the patients pose to society at large. We saw from our discussion of the readmittees that there is considerable threatening behavior and intimidation within the families of the mentally ill, but we want to extend and systematize those impressions to see which of the patients pose a threat to society and which do not. One of the important functions of the mental health system is to protect society from those persons who are mentally ill and dangerous, and one of the most common criticisms of the current system is that it no longer does that very well. We address this issue of threat and dangerousness by looking at the criminal activity of state patients and relating that activity to the clinical status of the patients.

Just as important as these two concerns is the third issue of whether aftercare (treatment outside the state hospitals) is effective. In relying on other agencies besides the state hospitals for treating the mentally ill, what kind of results are we getting? Do people who go into aftercare do better than those who do not? We answer that question in the next chapter. To address the first two concerns, we must look systematically at how the patients view their mental illness.

Patient Constructions of Mental Illness

One of the most important, and least understood, aspects of our new inclusionary system is the role of the patients' decisions in the treatment process. We can see—from the readmissions sample and the earlier discussion of how much help people received before they entered the state hospital—that many patients are not particularly interested in attending to their emotional problems in conventional clinical settings. Many do not receive clinical treatment; when they do, it is often slight. These facts, coupled with the obvious importance of the patient's desires in the treatment process, suggest that the patient's view of his or her illness plays a central role in determining what kind of help the patient seeks and how likely it is that he or she continues to treat the problem correctly. The cooperation of the patient is essential if the patient is to follow the treatment regimen recommended. Without that cooperation, community care is impossible.

For severe mental illnesses this problem is compounded by the problem of questionable volitional control by the patient. If cognitive and affective processes are distorted by mental illness, then rational models of adherence to health behaviors will no longer predict the patient's treatment and medication compliance. Indeed, we argue in this chapter that we must begin with the patient's subjective evaluation of the mental illness, that is, how he or she defines what is wrong, if we are to understand the health behavior in question. For example, if state mental patients see their problems in conventional medical terms, namely, that they suffer from an illness that can be treated with medical therapies, and that their doctor or other medical professional has both the authority and expertise to guide that treatment, then we should anticipate that the patients will follow the therapeutic regimen laid out for them, take their medication regularly, and return to the state hospital or other clinical setting when their symptoms are no longer manageable.

If, however, the patients do not think about their problems in medical terms, if they do not think anything is wrong with them, then one would hardly expect them to follow the regimen prescribed for them by people whose authority they do not accept. If there is nothing wrong, the treatment will seem irrelevant or be regarded as an infringement upon their freedom. These subjective evaluations may have seemed less relevant when the state hospitals kept patients for long periods and had a great deal of control over their treatment. Now the definitions patients give to their problems have far more serious consequences for the patients themselves as well as those around them.

We believe that in this more fluid inclusionary system, the medicalization of mental health problems will lead to better functioning in the community, for it constructs an explanatory scheme for patients that is connected to institutions (like the state hospitals) that attend to (or perhaps ameliorate) the patients' problems. A person who attributes his emotional problems to a severe mental illness would lower his own expectations of what he thinks he can accomplish in civil society. These lowered expectations would lead to fewer disappointments in life as he sets modest goals for himself and accomplishes them from time to time. While in past times, this medicalization of problems by others was treated as stigmatizing and deviant-producing, the process of self-labeling problems as illnesses might prove to be positive constructions of problematic behavior in an inclusionary system.

Those patients who do not think they have a problem or see that problem as existing outside their own mental processes (e.g., unemployment, the actions of a loved one, etc.) will continue to see aftercare and other mental health services as, at best, conveniences to be taken advantage of and, at worst, irrelevancies to their own problems. And perhaps most important, their own mental health may suffer, for they will continue to set goals for themselves that are difficult to reach and conflict with those around them, creating more stress for themselves and others and deteriorating in the process.

To examine the relationship of subjective evaluations of mental illness to overall mental health, we asked our sample of 313 state mental patients questions about how they thought about their problems. We relied on Kleinman's (1980) groundbreaking work on definitions of disease and illness in different cultures to construct measures that would capture these subjective evaluations of mental illness. After asking each patient what he or she calls the problem, we were able to create five categories of response that help clarify the relationship between these self-definitions and the patient's overall mental health. Our categories span the dimension of medicalization, from thinking one has no problem, to seeing that problem as due to external influences, to seeing one's problem as a function of how one behaves and thinks, to seeing the problem as the presence of mental illness. A fifth category was created for those patients who could not answer the question. We then assessed the relationship between the patient's definition of his problem and his overall mental health at the second interview.

The 313 mental patients in our sample were asked, "What do you call your problem?" "What name does it have?" Twenty-eight percent of the sample defined their problem in medical terms, using a specific diagnosis or trying to recall a diagnosis that would define their mental illness. In addition, 30 percent of people in our sample also named physical ailments, drug problems, personality defects, and behavior problems as the source of their troubles. Twenty-one percent saw other people or things, e.g., family members, friends, or lovers, as causing their problems and also specified concerns about everyday issues such as housing, money, and job problems. Another 16 percent of the sample said they had no problem.

In this analysis, we regressed all the measures of functioning (Global Assessment Scale; see below) on the independent measures of sex, race, age, education, diagnosis, and the person's explanatory model of his/her problem. We controlled for the time between the first and second interview and for all the functioning measures while the person was in the hospital. We also adjusted the variances for the variables we expected would have measurement error (education, diagnosis, and explanatory model). We compared the SADS and DMH diagnoses for assessing measurement error in diagnoses and compared Time 1 and Time 2 explanatory models of problem to get a measure of error for the explanatory model variables.

None of the independent measures we examined affects how people manage to care for themselves in the community (table 6–1). Thus, neither the person's explanatory model nor any other control variables such as education, gender, or race is related to his or her ability to manage everyday responsibilities. This is the case for all analyses that were corrected for measurement error.

The fact that people's capacity to perform everyday tasks does not improve over time can be attributed to the level of skills that the "Functioning Scale" measures. To measure functioning, we asked people to rate themselves as needing no help, some help, or a lot of help in completing ten basic living tasks and appropriate behaviors. A high score on the functioning scale indicates a low level of functioning. This scale is derived from questions in a similar study of community services to psychiatric patients (Solomon, Gordon, & Davis, 1984). The Cronbach's alpha for this scale was .7715. Substitutes for values missing from this scale were calculated by using a regression based on available information.

On the one hand, the scale measures those basic skills that almost everyone seems to learn early in life (table 6–2). Such skills are apparently so basic that they are not affected by variations in problem identification or social factors. On the other hand, the Functioning Scale also measures very complex skills, such as the ability to get aftercare services, finding things to do in one's spare time, or being able to hold a job. Many members of the sample are not able to do these things. These are complex, and difficult activities, requiring the completion of a number of preparatory activities. For example, getting aftercare means the person is aware that aftercare is available to him/her and can mobilize his/her behaviors to find an agency, make an appointment, and then get to that agency for the appointment.

That the people in this sample do not change in terms of managing their lives according to the Functioning Scale reflects the fact that they have learned the basics of self-care but cannot manage the further skills necessary to get them out of their sheltered environments. Their inability to manage money, get aftercare, and act appropriately in many social situations suggests that they lack the more complex skills needed to function as conventional members of society.

What People Do

The list of twenty-five activities used to measure what people do with their time in the community is one means of assessing the quality of people's lives once they are released from the hospital. To measure daily activities, we asked people to respond yes or no to twenty-five activities that they may have participated in during the last week (table 6–3). A high score on the activities scale indicates a high level of weekly activity. The Cronbach's alpha for this scale was .7742.

People turned out to be more active in the hospital than in the community. A high activity level is positively related to being diagnosed as character disordered (the least severe diagnosis). The less mentally disabled may be most active because they have the capacity to mobilize their behaviors to do more things than people diagnosed as schizophrenic or manic-depressive. Age is negatively related to activity level, but as we adjusted for measurement error in our analyses, the effects of age on activity level decreased, while the effects of being diagnosed as character disordered increased. In sum, the combination of youth and the absence of severe mental disability is associated with high levels of activity.

Being active is not related to problem identification nor to any of the other control variables. Activity levels for our sample are simply a function of being able to perform the activities, i.e., being young and not severely mentally handicapped. Almost everyone in the sample listened to radio, watched television, walked, or just sat and thought. To be more active than most people in the study, one has

Table 6–1. The MHPP Sample: Relationship Between Patients' Characteristics and Functioning Ability

Independent Measures	GAS		Function		Activity		Readmissions	
	B	Sig	B	Sig	B	Sig	B	Sig
Controls								
GAS	.072	ns	−.001	ns	−.006	ns	−.019	.05
Active	−.143	ns	−.059	ns	.284	.00	−.015	ns
Number of previous admissions	−.110	ns	−.033	ns	.027	ns	.055	.00
Function	−1.182	.00	.409	.00	−.016	ns	−.010	ns
Independent Measures								
Sex	4.350	.07	−.509	ns	.461	ns	−.190	ns
Age	.073	ns	−.026	ns	−.047	.05	−.032	.00
Education	.785	.05	−.091	ns	.119	ns	−.049	ns
White	−2.990	ns	−.780	ns	−.303	ns	−.041	ns

	B		B		B		B	
Other race	5.778	ns	1.162	ns	.601	ns	-.504	ns
Affective disordered	3.572	ns	.035	ns	.066	ns	-.004	ns
Character disordered	4.754	ns	-1.003	ns	1.491	.09	.897	.02
Internal nonpsych	-7.000	.04	.260	ns	-.334	ns	.138	ns
External problem	-9.384	.03	-.069	ns	-.356	ns	-.058	ns
No problem	-7.044	ns	-.279	ns	-.079	ns	-.558	ns
Missing data on Explanatory Model	-25.522	.00	.081	ns	-1.932	ns	-.021	ns
Time in study	-.002	ns	.001	ns	-.000	ns	.000	.05
Constant	61.34354		12.29100		6.90181		3.15442	
	F=3.14		F=3.52		F=3.32		F=3.84	
	df=207		df=207		df=207		df=207	
	p<.00		p<.00		p<.00		p<.00	

B=unstandardized regression coefficient.

Table 6–2. The MHPP Sample: Managing Everyday Living

| Variable Name | Uncorrected | Extent of Attenuation for Measurement Error | |
| | | Unstandardized Regression Coefficients | |
		Small Correction	Large Correction
Function (T1)	0.43195**	0.40931**	0.40890**
Activity (T1)	−0.06383	−0.05924	−0.05926
GAS (T1)	−0.00165	−0.00057	−0.00108
Previous admission	−0.03780	−0.03283	−0.03295
Gender	−0.66644	−0.50858	−0.50309
White	−0.97937	−0.78003	−0.78155
Other race	1.22545	1.16230	1.15330
Age	−0.01858	−0.02567	−0.02581
Education	−0.08365	−0.09081	−0.09046
Affective dis.	0.19237	0.03515	0.03099
Character dis.	−0.93121	−1.00337	−0.99231
Nonpsych. prob.	0.20553	0.25952	0.28455
External prob.	−0.04303	−0.06887	−0.07218
No prob.	−0.07557	−0.27857	−0.32126
Missing prob.	0.06951	0.08099	0.09708
Time in study	0.00637*	0.00061	0.00061
Constant	10.26230	12.29100	12.31342

$**p < .01$ $F = 3.91597**$ $F = 3.52357**$ $F = 3.52687**$
$*p < .10$ df = 16 df = 16 df = 16
R square = .24701 R square = .22790 R square = .22806

to perform such complex activities as going to a sports event, going to a library, taking a class, or doing volunteer work. Thus, one who is severely mentally impaired cannot engage in many of the activities mentioned in the scale.

Overall Mental Health

The Global Assessment Scale (GAS) is a measure that evaluates the overall mental health of a person on a number

Table 6–3. The MHPP Sample: Activity after Release

	Extent of Attenuation for Measurement Error		
	Unstandardized Regression Coefficients		
Variable Name	Uncorrected	Small Correction	Large Correction
Function (T1)	−0.00561	−0.01585	−0.03831
Activity (T1)	0.30288**	0.28418**	0.27868**
GAS (T1)	−0.00414	−0.00556	−0.00224
Previous admission	0.03043	0.02727	0.02334
Gender	0.36476	0.46136	0.41916
White	−0.26228	−0.30250	−0.42541
Other race	0.57690	0.60131	0.63453
Age	0.05530*	−0.04729*	−0.04014
Education	0.10744	0.11862	0.10988
Affective dis.	−0.04104	0.06570	−0.05655
Character dis.	1.26565*	1.49118*	1.52680*
Nonpsych. prob.	−0.36526	−0.33403	−1.04746
External prob.	−0.13880	−0.39594	−1.28853
No prob.	0.19470	0.07862	−0.90175
Missing prob.	−1.63896	−1.93236	−3.13261
Time in study	−0.00172	−0.00018	−0.00019
Constant	7.28907	6.90181	7.82552

p<.01   F=3.60109   F=3.32316**   F=3.39272**
*p<.10   df=16   df=16   df=16
    R square=.23175   R square=.21776   R square=.22131

of criteria—e.g., extent of symptomatology, social effectiveness, and life satisfaction—yet provides a single estimate of mental health. During a specific time period, it rates a person's psychological health from 1 (the psychologically sickest person) to 100 (the psychologically healthiest). The GAS rating measures overall severity of psychiatric condition on the basis of three principal dimensions: proportion of life sectors affected by impairment, loss of reality testing, and danger posed to life. The defining characteristics of each ten-point interval on the scale are described on the rating form. For example, a person falling in the range of 51 to 60 would show:

Moderate symptoms or generally functioning with some difficulty (e.g., few friends and flat affect, depressed mood and pathological self-doubt, euphoric mood and pressure of speech; moderately severe anti-social behavior).

At the end of the Time 2 interview, raters were instructed to choose the ten-point range bracketing the subject's lowest level of functioning during the week. They were then instructed to choose a specific number within that continuum that best represented the subject's health. The result is a continuous rating of subject functioning standardized from absolute sickness to absolute health.

The raters for the scale were trained by a team of two clinical psychologists in a ten-hour training course concerning symptom definition and rating, interviewing techniques, reliability exercises, and videotaped exercises of actual interviews (Endicott, Spitzer, Fleiss, & Cohen, 1976).

The patients in the sample averaged a score of 32 points on the GAS while they were in the hospital and 52 points while they were in the community. Although their overall mental health improved in the community, they were still considered to be highly symptomatic, requiring treatment and attention.

Being female and better educated is associated with better mental health. Women score an average of five points higher on the GAS than men, and each year of education is associated with almost a one-point increase in the GAS rating (table 6–4).

The lack of a medical understanding of one's problems is related to poor mental health. People who could not or would not name their problem score lower on the GAS than people who define their problem in any other way. Those people who defined their problems in psychiatric terms scored an average of seventeen points higher on the GAS than people who could not name their troubles. People who define their troubles as imposed on them by some external conditions, such as family, and people who define their troubles in terms of personality problems or physical ailments score lower on the GAS than people who define their troubles in psychiatric terms. This finding suggests that how one thinks about emotional problems is important to overall mental health.

The effects of education and being female become insignificant

Table 6–4. The MHPP Sample: Overall Mental Health

Variable Name	Extent of Attenuation for Measurement Error		
	Unstandardized Regression Coefficients		
	Uncorrected	Small Correction	Large Correction
Function (T1)	−1.13311**	−1.18172**	−1.71387**
Activity (T1)	−0.06069	−0.14250	−0.25086
GAS (T1)	0.06218	0.07285	0.13340
Previous admission	−0.06160	−0.10967	−0.20328
Gender	5.41848*	4.34655*	3.50602
White	−0.88477	−2.99025	−5.76753*
Other race	5.65806	5.77763	6.37303*
Age	−0.03409	0.07289	0.22872*
Education	0.74604*	0.78513*	0.56605
Affective dis.	2.50134	3.57162	0.50580
Character dis.	3.17943	4.75429	5.96758
Nonpsych. prob.	−2.97257	−7.00012*	−23.66399**
External prob.	−3.84524	−9.38419*	−30.29442**
No prob.	−1.75866	−7.04435	−31.60541**
Missing prob.	−16.79525*	−25.52194**	−51.19836**
Time in study	−0.01376	−0.00140	−0.00174
Constant	62.75990	61.34354	84.02857

p<.01 F=2.84439 F=3.13894** F=4.59073**
*p<.10 df=16 df=16 df=16
R square=.19242 R square=.20820 R square=.27775

when we control for measurement error, while the effects of race and age become significant. In this analysis, we find that whites score lower on the GAS than any other racial category and that older people score higher on the GAS. This means that the variance that is attributed to being female and well-educated is shared by the variances of being a racial minority and being older. Among the blacks there are proportionately more women than men than in the entire sample, and these women tend to be older than the men in our study. Thus, the positive correlation between being female, black, and old affects the significance levels of our unstandardized regression coefficients of gender and education.

Given this analysis, life in the community is an extension of life in the institution, which, we suspect, is a continuation of one's previous life in the community. In other words, there is a great deal of continuity and constancy in the lives of mental patients, regardless of the situation they find themselves in on any given day. How one will act tomorrow will in the main be predicted by how one acts today, especially because our inclusionary mental health system has shrunk the differences between hospital and community settings and the periods of time spent in each of them. While the activities and functioning levels remain fairly constant over time, there is some evidence that the way one views one's mental illness does have an effect on one's overall mental health. The state patient's mental health does depend on how one thinks about one's problems, and a medical label is related to better mental health.

The adult mental patient, like most adults in our society, has a fairly constant approach to life and a well-established way of coping with everyday problems. While there is always the possibility of change and growth, realizing much of that potential depends on the strength of the interventions or services with which the person comes in contact. If the person is to learn new ways of doing things and develop improved capacities to function, those interventions will have to create strong incentives for change and the resources to influence how the patient goes about daily activities. We now recognize that the hospital has changed profoundly in its goals and capacities to influence patients. Shorter stays and the objective of returning the patient to the community as quickly as possible make the potential effect of hospitalization rather modest. In the next chapter we turn to community treatment and aftercare to see whether these interventions have the capacity to change the lives of state mental patients.

7 LIFE IN THE COMMUNITY: DOES HELP HELP?

Perhaps the most important consequence of the transformation of the mental health system from an exclusionary to an inclusionary system is the blurring of institutional-community boundaries. When the mental health system was exclusionary, there was a distinct threshold between being cared for in an institution and living in the community. There were major differences between being in and being out. Social scientists, especially the radicals, saw entering the hospital as the beginning of a "betrayal funnel," in which the innocent were recruited to the status of mental patient (Goffman, 1961). Institutional theories of the self, which set the tone for the debate about deinstitutionalization, were premised on the negative effects of being in a state hospital. Psychiatric theory, while more sanguine about institutions, was no less adamant about the importance of exclusion. The idea of the therapeutic community played a major role in supporting exclusionary care and highlighted the chasm between being inside and being out.

If our analysis of the contemporary state hospital and those who use it is persuasive, then it should be clear that our inclusionary system is inconsistent with this sharp demarcation between the community and the hospital. The community now provides places where the mentally ill live and are served and which have some, if not all, of the aspects of an institution (nursing homes, general hospitals, private institutions, etc.), while the hospital itself no longer cuts the patient off from the community. Hospital stays are shorter, civil rights are respected (more than they used to be), and the ease of movement back and forth between the hospital and the community removes much of the isolation that characterized the old state hospital. As community living takes on aspects of the exclusionary hospital in various settings, and the hospital becomes more like the places the patients stay when in the community, the old distinctions become less sharp.

The blurring of the lines between hospital and community in

the inclusionary system demands that a discussion of aftercare or community living begin with new concepts that take this change into consideration. The old approach—built on mental health exceptionalism and guild innovationism—formulated the issues of aftercare as problems of having the appropriate services in place and getting the person to the right clinical setting upon release. This meant that hospital care should be followed by a matching process that found the clinically appropriate community care for the patient. If linkages were made, then the problem of aftercare had been solved. A return to the hospital was the result of either a lack of aftercare options or a mismatch between the clinical needs of the patient and the available clinical service. Much of the debate about how to improve care has focused on creating clinical services that will provide the support patients need to remain out of the hospital.

But what if hospitalization does not represent a radical separation of the patient from his or her surroundings? What if, for a substantial subset of those who go to the state hospital, the hospital is on a continuum of places to obtain help in the face of limited resources? What if so-called aftercare services are supplements rather than alternatives to the hospital care? That would mean that the "after" in aftercare misrepresents the relationship between the community care and the hospital care, since the patients move back and forth between the settings in accordance with their needs and the wishes of those who run the programs. It would also suggest that the relations between the hospital and the community services are characterized more by cooperation and mutual benefit than isolation and misunderstanding. It is this new picture that better represents how the inclusionary system of care works in Chicago. And it is this new picture that we describe in this chapter.

We have seen in the previous chapters that the lives of the mentally ill outside the state hospital are shaped by the lack of financial and clinical resources. Many patients return to state hospitals when symptoms flare or when conflict emerges within families or at agencies. The state hospital has become one of the few places they or their families can turn to when troubles mount. That, of course, was not the way it was supposed to be with the advent of community care. Patients who were outside the state hospital were supposed to have a variety of services available to them in order to avoid rehospitalization, from residential services to less intrusive clinical programs, that helped the patient cope with problems and, it was hoped, improved his or her clinical status. Those services were supposed to be provided in most jurisdictions by private agencies and organizations that were paid by the state. In contemporary American style, public financing and private initiative were joined to solve a social problem. The state provides the money, and private industry (in this case, the human service industry) provides the service. Where these services are and whom they serve, while influenced by the state, are determined by the private organization itself.

Our reliance on the private sector for the provision of this service creates serious problems that are just now becoming visible. First, we must rely on organizations with acceptable track records in the responsible administration of clinical services. There are few of these organizations operating in any given jurisdiction with the expertise and interest to be involved in the delivery of services. This lack of private vendors creates a situation in which the buyer of the service (the state) has to depend on a few vendors and must meet their needs in order to involve them. It also means that the services have to be delivered in places and ways that are acceptable to the vendors.

Since many private organizations have customers other than the state, the state must meet certain requirements in order to contract with them for the service the state wishes to have offered. This creates a difficult situation for the state, because it must compromise with the private organizations over a variety of issues, including who is served, at what levels, and for how long a period. These problems are compounded by the separation of the purchaser of service (the State of Illinois) from the consumer of service (the mental patient) in this public marketplace. Since patients use their own criteria for deciding which services to utilize, and under what conditions, and since the private organizations usually exercise a great deal of discretion as to whom they treat and for how long, the purchaser of the services has little control over what is consumed and by whom.

These factors in the community create a service environment in which care is a matter of personal choice for the patient and the provider. If the agency does not want to treat the person, it can and does send him back to the state hospital or releases him. The state has little control over these decisions and can only try to review them through the information it receives from the agency.

The rhetoric of community care revolves around the assumption that the better the care, the less likely it is that the person will have to return to the hospital. We have seen in the case of many of the readmittees that receiving care in the community can lead to a readmission. For those who see themselves as mentally ill, community care would seem to make sense as something that would be sought. Thus, patients who define their problem in medical terms would be more likely to seek aftercare than those who do not think they have a problem. We will also show that medication compliance is related to fewer readmissions. We argue that the cognitive dimension of how the patient defines his or her problem will be the link to aftercare attendance and that once linked, taking one's medication keeps one out of the hospital.

A fundamental belief of the community mental health movement was that people should and would receive services in the community. We examine first the use of community services by patients discharged from Chicago-area state mental hospitals and then the relationship between service use and readmissions to state hospitals. While previous studies have suggested that aftercare clinics reduce recidivism, it is not clear whether that reduction is due to the medication offered to clients, to other services, or to the type of patient who attends aftercare (Anthony, Buell, Sharratt, & Althoff, 1972). Here we examine the relationship between each of these factors and readmissions in order to identify the ameliorative effects, if any, of community care.

Data for this discussion come from a questionnaire mailed to aftercare agencies. During the second interview (Time 2), patients were asked whether they received aftercare services from anyone and whether they lived in a residential care facility. Of the 210 patients interviewed at Time 2, 144 responded yes. Of these 144 people, 23 mentioned two agencies. Therefore, a total of 167 questionnaires were distributed, 113 of which were returned, for a response rate of 67 percent, considerably higher than the usual response rate of 10–50 percent for mailed surveys. Nine of these questionnaires were returned uncompleted, the agency indicating that it did not know the person or did not have records that would enable it to complete the survey. Thus, 104 completed questionnaires about 91 people were returned from 50 different agencies. (The agency that had provided more services is considered the "primary" agency in the discussion below.)

Table 7–1. The MHPP Sample: Demographic Characteristics of Those Receiving Aftercare

	Survey Returned N=99	Survey Not Returned N=45	
Race			
Black	47.5%	62.2%	χ^2=10.3729
White	47.5	22.2	df=2
Other	5.1	15.6	p=.0056
Previous Admissions			
0	28.3	35.6	χ^2=3.8754
1–5	41.4	24.4	df=2
6+	30.3	40.0	ns
Age			
18–34	63.6	71.1	χ^2=1.3828
35–49	24.2	15.6	df=2
50–65	12.1	13.3	ns
Sex			
Male	59.6	64.4	χ^2=0.1360
Female	40.4	35.6	df=1
			ns
Yearly Income			
Less than $3,001	40.2	50.0	χ^2=2.0097
$3,001-$6,000	37.8	25.0	df=2
More than $6,000	22.0	25.0	ns

Table 7–1 compares those for whom we have aftercare information with those who said they attended aftercare but for whom surveys were not completed. There are no significant demographic differences between these groups by number of previous admissions, age, sex, or income. The only significant difference was by race, with fewer surveys about black and other clients returned completed (47.5 percent and 5.1 percent, respectively, versus 47.5 percent for whites).

We also compared patients on self-reported scales concerning

Table 7–2. The MHPP Sample: Functioning Ability of Those Receiving Aftercare

	Survey Returned (N=99)	Survey Not Returned (N=45)	
Functioning			
Low	45.5%	37.8%	$\chi^2=0.4635$
High	54.5	62.2	df=1
			ns
Activity Level			
Low	51.5	51.1	$\chi^2=0.0000$
High	48.5	48.9	df=1
Interaction			
Low	48.5	53.3	$\chi^2=0.1293$
High	51.5	46.7	df=1
			ns
GAS Rating			
Low	46.6	47.5	$\chi^2=0.0000$
High	53.4	52.5	df=1
			ns

their functioning, daily activities, levels of interaction with family and friends, and Global Assessment Scale (GAS) ratings that were assigned during Time 2 of the larger study.

The findings presented in table 7–2 indicate no differences in functioning, activity levels, interaction levels, or GAS ratings between those whose surveys were returned and those whose surveys were not completed by aftercare staff.

Who Gets Community Care?

The reduction in readmissions found by previous studies of community care users may be due to differences between those who receive community care and those who do not. It is possible that those who attend community care function better than those who do not, and that differences in readmission rates are due to differences between these two groups and not to the effects of community care services. In order to examine this possibility, we compared those patients in our study who responded yes when asked whether they received community care services to those who responded no (table 7–3). The results indicate that those who receive community care do not differ significantly from those who do not in race, number of previous admissions, age, gender, yearly income, functioning levels, amount of activity and interaction, or GAS rating of mental health. This suggests that it is not the case that community care agencies are serving those who are less disabled by mental illness, thus accounting for differences in readmission rates between community care attenders and those who do not attend.

Linkage with Community Care Agencies

In 80 percent of the cases, the patient was referred to the agency by a psychiatric hospital or by the psychiatric unit of a general hospital, and in 88.9 percent of these cases, the patient kept the first appointment. Thus, the linkage procedures, which require that patients be assigned to an agency upon discharge from the hospital, appear to be a primary route to care for those who received services. We found no relationship between the type of contact that the agency made with the client before discharge (e.g., by phone, agency visiting client, client visiting agency, etc.) and whether the first appointment was kept ($\chi^2=2.3608$; df=2; p=.3072).

Sixty-nine of these clients were still being seen at the agency at the time the survey was completed; twelve had withdrawn from the program or moved out of the residential facility. In only one case had the agency terminated services for a client. The length of time that the patients had received services typically was at least six months, and for almost half the sample, more than a year (table 7–4). (In cases where people had attended more than one agency, only the primary agency is included in the tables.)

Many (76 percent) patients in this sample are young (18–34) and rely on their parents or other family members in times of trouble

Table 7–3. The MHPP Sample: Demographic and Functioning Characteristics of Those Receiving Community Care

	Community Care	No Community Care	
Race			
Black	53.0%	65.2%	χ^2=3.9861
White	39.6	23.9	df=2
Other	7.3	10.9	ns
Previous Admissions			
0	28.0	41.3	χ^2=3.3068
1–5	34.1	23.9	df=2
6+	37.8	34.8	ns
Age			
18–34	65.9	73.9	χ^2=1.2664
35–49	23.2	19.6	df=2
50–65	11.0	6.5	ns
Sex			
Male	63.4	65.2	χ^2=0.0026
Female	36.6	34.8	df=1
Yearly Income			
Less than $3,001	42.9	54.5	χ^2=2.4406
$3,001–$6,000	34.3	31.8	df=2
More than $6,000	22.9	13.6	ns
GAS Rating			
Low	45.3	53.5	χ^2=0.6034
High	54.7	46.5	df=1
Functioning			
Low	44.5	41.3	χ^2=0.0481
High	55.5	58.7	df=1
Activity			
Low	53.7	56.5	χ^2=0.0313
High	46.3	43.5	df=1
Interaction			
Low	52.4	43.5	χ^2=0.8233
High	47.6	56.5	df=1
			ns

Table 7-4. The MHPP Sample: Length of Time in Aftercare

	N	Percent
Less than 3 months	9	10.0
3–5 months	10	11.1
6–11 months	27	30.0
1–2 years	23	25.6
More than 2 years	21	23.3
Total	90*	

*Data missing for one case.

(Lewis et al., 1987). To examine the extent to which community care agencies involve the families of patients, we asked the agency to indicate whether it gave education or support directly to the family or involved the family in the patient's treatment. In twenty cases, no family was available; data were missing for four cases. Table 7–5 shows that in the remaining sixty-three cases, the most frequent form of family involvement was monitoring of the patient by the family. (Table 7–6 shows that only 16 percent of the cases received family therapy.)

We found no significant relationships between the family items and the functioning scale, the GAS ratings, the activity scale, or the interaction scale.

Table 7-5. The MHPP Sample: Family Involvement in Aftercare (N=63)*

Family monitors and reports on client	71.0%
Family educated about mental illness	57.5
Family monitors and reports on medication	46.0
Agency supports family	44.7
Parents group	1.0

*Total is more than 100 percent because families could be involved in more than one way.

Table 7–6. The MHPP Sample: Psychotherapeutic Aftercare

Type of Service	Percentage Receiving Service	Number of Weeks Per 12 Months (avg.*)	Number of Sessions Per Week (avg.*)	Avg. length of session* (minutes)
Individual therapy	75	26.50	1.2	50
Case management	58	30.30	1.7	53
Milieu therapy	31	40.50	4.8	400
Group therapy	28	27.75	1.8	63
Vocational training	21	23.60	2.7	169
Medication group	17	21.65	.8	49
Family therapy	16	15.67	.9	55
Self-help	15	29.50	2.3	74
Day treatment	12	33.67	4.0	282
Educational counseling	9	22.75	1.9	70
Substance abuse group	8	25.00	1.5	58

*Averages were computed only for those receiving the service; those not receiving the service were excluded from the average.

Those patients who do receive community care make a connection with the community care agency through referral from a hospital; they are likely to keep the first appointment, and continue in community care for six months or more. Almost half (48.9 percent) have remained in community care for over a year. Thus, these patients constitute a group of steady users of community care services, both before and after a hospitalization.

Type of Services Received

We asked about three types of services that agencies could provide to clients. The first type involved training or assistance

Table 7–7. The MHPP Sample: Aftercare Help in Daily Living Skills (N=91)

	None	Assistance	Training
Appropriate social behavior	15.6%	36.7%	47.8%
Use leisure time	19.1	43.8	37.1
Meeting basic needs (food, etc.)	23.6	39.3	37.1
Managing financial affairs	35.6	42.5	21.8
Using community resources	39.6	27.5	33.0
Help with role responsibilities	40.4	22.5	37.1
Household tasks	58.9	17.8	23.3
Handling legal affairs	71.6	18.2	10.2

in daily living skills; the second type of service involved ongoing psychotherapeutic care; the third type included intermittent or emergency care. Measures were adapted in part from the Uniform Client Data Instrument (Goldstrom & Manderscheid, 1982) and a study conducted by Solomon et al. (1984).

HELP WITH DAILY LIVING SKILLS

Agency staff indicated whether patients received assistance, training, or no help for each item. As table 7–7 indicates, the most training was provided for appropriate social behavior, while the least was provided for handling legal affairs, financial affairs, and household tasks. Since handling household tasks is necessary for independent living, it is surprising that so little attention is paid to this skill by community care agencies. Overall, the last column of table 7–7 indicates that fewer than half the patients received training in any of the daily living skills.

PSYCHOTHERAPEUTIC SERVICES

Table 7–6 shows the percentage of patients receiving a variety of psychotherapeutic services. What is striking about this table is the narrow range of services received by the clients. The most common

Table 7–8. The MHPP Sample: Emergency or Intermittent Aftercare Services

Wrote prescription for oral medication	70.8%
Crisis assistance	67.0
Monitored for tardive dyskinesia	65.9
Filled prescription for oral medication	60.7
Gave injectable medication	24.1
Located community housing	21.1
Placed in sheltered work	19.8
Provided emergency housing	14.5
Psychological testing	13.5
Provided apartment	11.6
Provided group home	7.2
Placed in competitive work	3.3

psychotherapeutic service received was individual therapy; the next most common was case management. While at least half of the sample received these two services, fewer than a third received any other psychotherapeutic service.

Tables 7–6 and 7–7 together suggest that patients who do receive community care receive fairly traditional forms of service—individual therapy or case management. That is, there is little evidence of widespread use of psychosocial rehabilitation in the form of training in daily living skills or the use of group support techniques, such as a medication group.

EMERGENCY OR INTERMITTENT SERVICES

The third type of services is offered occasionally or in an emergency. Table 7–8 summarizes these services.

To explore the nature of the crisis assistance, we asked whether the agency provided emergency medication and/or psychological intervention to prevent rehospitalization for this patient. No such need arose in 19.5 percent of the cases, and 12.6 percent of the agencies replied no. In 35.6 percent of the cases, assistance was

Table 7–9. The MHPP Sample: Medications Used

Anti-psychotic	63.2%
Mood stabilizer	11.8
Anti-side effect	9.2
Antidepressant	6.6
Anticonvulsant	3.9
Anti-anxiety	2.6
Other	2.6

provided and prevented hospitalization, while in 32.2 percent, such crisis assistance had been provided but the rehospitalization occurred anyway.

COMPLIANCE WITH MEDICATION

The positive relationship found in previous studies between community care attendance and lower admission rates may be due to the administration of medication by community care agencies rather than the provision of other services. We therefore examined the role of medication in services provided to patients, especially because the writing and filling of medication prescriptions and monitoring for tardive dyskinesia are services provided to many patients (see above). Eighty-one of the patients in this study took psychotropic medication. The results overall show a U-shaped curve for medication compliance: 27.3 percent of patients are low in compliance (take their medications rarely or not at all); 46.8 percent take them almost always; 26 percent take them all the time. Thus, the majority of patients who are in community care comply with drug regimens. The percentages of patients taking specific types of medication are presented in table 7–9. In 61.6 percent of the cases, the patient's medication was paid for by public aid or Medicaid; in 16.3 percent of the cases, the agency paid. Only 7.7 percent of clients paid for their own medication.

Agency staff reported several reasons for noncompliance (table 7–10). The most frequently mentioned reason was that the patient did not see him/herself as ill and needing medication.

Table 7–10. The MHPP Sample: Reasons for Not Taking Medications

Patient not seeing self as ill	62.2%
Patient not understanding need for medication	55.3
Intolerable side effects	21.6
Too much medication prescribed	5.4
Family discouraged medication	0

The Relationship of Community Care and Readmissions

Of the ninety people whose surveys were returned from community care services (missing data on one person), 42.2 percent had returned to the hospital in the six months following discharge from the hospital. As nearly half the sample had been in community care for more than a year, this means they had been in community care before or during the time of their hospitalization at Time 1 of the study. We looked at the relationship between community care use and readmission to the hospital for all those interviewed at Time 2.

Of those readmitted, 25.9 percent did not receive community care while 74.1 percent did. Thus, for a sizeable proportion of those receiving aftercare, these services appear to complement or overlap with hospitalization. Of those not readmitted, 81.3 percent received aftercare while 18.7 percent did not. However, the relationship between receiving community care and residential services and being readmitted to the hospital in the six months after discharge was not significant ($\chi^2 = 1.135$, df=1).

The relationship between length of attendance in aftercare and readmissions approaches significance ($\chi^2 = 7.35$, df=3, p=.06) (table 7–11). The longer one is in community care, the less likely is readmission.

In order to examine the relationship between family involvement and readmissions, we combined the family items into an additive scale (Cronbach's alpha = .67), and then divided the scale into low

Table 7–11. The MHPP Sample: Percentage Readmitted by Length of Attendance in Community Care

	Readmitted	
Attendance	No	Yes
Less than 6 months	12%	34.3%
6–11 months	26	28.6
1–2 years	32	20.0
2+ years	30	17.0

and high categories on the basis of frequency distributions. The relationship between family involvement and readmissions is not significant, although the frequencies indicate that more family involvement may be associated with fewer readmissions (table 7–12).

A similar procedure was followed to examine the relationship between receiving assistance or training in daily living skills and readmission to the hospital (table 7–13). Cronbach's alpha for the assistance scale is .83. This relationship also was not significant ($\chi^2=.30$, df=1).

No significant relationships were found between receipt of each of these psychotherapeutic services and readmission. While for many of the services, the lack of significance may be due to the low numbers of people who received the services, even the two most

Table 7–12. The MHPP Sample: Relationship Between Family Involvement and Incidence of Rehospitalization

	Readmitted	
Family Involvement	No	Yes
Low	38.9%	53.6%
High	61.1	46.4

Table 7–13. The MHPP Sample: Relationship Between Help with Daily Living Skills and Incidence of Rehospitalization

	Readmitted	
Amount of Assistance	No	Yes
Low	50.0%	58.3%
High	50.0	41.7

frequent services, case management and individual therapy, were not significantly related to readmissions (χ^2=.000, df=1; χ^2=.08, df=1, respectively).

Table 7–14 presents the relationship between compliance with medication regimen and readmissions. This relationship is significant (χ^2=6.88, df=2, p=.03). Of those readmitted, 42.4 percent were low in medication compliance, while only 15.9 percent of those not readmitted fell into this category.

Table 7–15 presents the relationship between monitoring for tardive dyskinesia and readmissions (χ^2=6.32, df=1, p=.011). Of those who were not readmitted, 76 percent had been monitored and 24 percent had not.

In a similar study conducted in Cleveland (Solomon et al., 1984), the variety of services received by the client was the best predictor

Table 7–14. The MHPP Sample: Relationship Between Medication Compliance (as Reported by Aftercare Agency) and Incidence of Rehospitalization

	Readmitted	
Compliance	No	Yes
Poor	15.9%	42.4%
Moderate	52.3	39.4
Excellent	31.8	18.2

Table 7–15. The MHPP Sample: Relationship Between Agency Monitoring for Tardive Dyskinesia and Incidence of Readmission (N=86)

	Readmitted	
Monitored	No	Yes
No	24.0%	52.8%
Yes	76.0	47.2

of readmission to the hospital. Those who received a greater diversity of services were less likely to return to the hospital. In our study the relationship between receiving a variety of services and likelihood of return to the hospital was not significant ($\chi^2 = .68$, df=1), perhaps because the range of services received was so limited.

In sum, the factors that appear to be significantly related to reduced readmissions are those associated with medication compliance. Other services do not seem to be related to reduced readmissions, although the small numbers of people who received some of these services make it difficult to test this conclusively.

The services most commonly received by patients are case management, individual therapy, and medication—the writing and filling of prescriptions for oral medications and monitoring for tardive dyskinesia. Less than half of the patients in the sample received training in daily living skills or group support techniques. While many received individual therapy, the patients' view of this experience (in our qualitative data) focuses not so much on the treatment as on having someone listen to them. The supportive aspect of this experience may be the critical dimension of therapy for them, but one that may not affect rehospitalization.

When we examined the relationship between services and readmission to the hospital, we found that significant relationships concerned medication. Those who comply with medication regimens and are monitored for tardive dyskinesia are less likely to be readmitted. The lack of significant relationships with some of the services may be due to the low numbers of patients receiving those services, but the overall pattern seems clear. With the exception of medication, community care services may be desired by patients and improve the quality of their lives, but they do not necessarily keep them out of the hospital.

Indeed, there may very well be a complicated relationship between community care, readmissions, and medication compliance. An unwillingness to comply with medication requirements may increase the number and/or severity of symptoms at the same time that it gets the patient in trouble with those around him or her. The combination of the two factors may increase the likelihood of being readmitted.

8 IDENTIFYING TYPES OF CRIMINAL STATE MENTAL PATIENTS

The inclusionary mental health system has transformed the lives of mental patients and those who care for them. The problem of criminality of mental patients illustrates this transformation. Thirty years ago, when mental patients were excluded from civil society by hospitalization, their very segregation made criminality a management problem for hospital personnel rather than a police problem for the communities in which the patients live. Involuntary commitment was the primary mechanism used by the state to hospitalize those patients whose behavior was problematic. The current system no longer relies on involuntary commitment. Over 97 percent of all admissions to Chicago-area state hospitals are now voluntary, and the average length of stay is about a week. Clearly, the state hospital no longer deals with the problem of criminality by incarcerating dangerous patients, and the problem of patient criminality exhibited in the community has no easy solution for either policy makers or researchers.

In this chapter, we explore the issue of patient criminality in order to ascertain how much criminality state patients exhibit and what types of crimes they commit. We also explore the relationship between the types of criminality exhibited and the clinical profiles of patients. We demonstrate that there are three types of criminal mental patients; each poses challenges to the mental health and criminal justice agencies that must cope with their behavior.

The issue of criminality among state mental patients also illustrates the inadequacies of traditional categories of debate about mental health policy. The tendency to homogenize the mentally ill and exceptionalize their problems has made criminality a source of differences between groups for most researchers. While research on group comparisons is useful, it cannot replace careful studies of state mental patients' disorders that examine the probability that they will commit crimes. We must observe the variations within the group; **109** for it is this approach that will assist those charged with controlling violence.

The director of the National Institute of Justice, in the introduction to a research note on *Crime and Mental Disorder* (Monahan & Steadman, 1984), cautions the reader on the limits of this type of research. "Unless we do a better job distinguishing among the mentally ill, we do a disservice to those recovering from mental illness or whose mental health problems pose no risk to others. And we risk obscuring the real issue: criminal conduct and the threat to victims."

For more than fifty years, researchers have debated whether mental patients are more criminal than the general population (Rabkin, 1979). Despite a wealth of empirical efforts to study the criminality of the mentally disordered, previous investigations provide scanty knowledge about the precise nature of criminal behavior among mental patients. Traditional designs and analytic strategies that draw upon aggregate arrest data to compare mental patients against normals (Ashley, 1922; Brill & Malzberg, 1962; Cohen & Freeman, 1945; Durbin, Pasewark, & Albers, 1977; Giovannoni & Gurel, 1967; Pollock, 1938; Rappeport & Lassen, 1965; Zitrin, Hardesty, & Burdock, 1976) obscure important differences among patients who commit crimes. Perhaps the most telling criticism of prior research on this topic is that it reflects the implicit and unsupported assumption that mental patients are alike with respect to their criminal tendencies and activities. Although past studies have detailed the different types of crimes committed by patients, they have failed to distinguish between the different types of patients committing those crimes (Sosowsky, 1980). Hence, we are left with the false impression that all mental patients are either more or less dangerous or criminal than the general population.

Teplin (1984, 1985) was one of the first to note the limitations of aggregate arrest data in examining the criminality of the mentally disordered. By presenting first-hand evidence about encounters between the police and the mentally ill, Teplin's studies are a major advance over earlier research; however, her efforts also suffer from some shortcomings. Specifically, Teplin's observational studies rely on immediately visible and public episodes of criminal behavior in which an offender is present. Such instances encompass a tiny fraction of all criminal activity and represent a handful of incidents involving less serious crimes. Moreover, it is not clear from her studies whether individuals regarded as mentally disturbed are actually mental patients. In addition, similar to research employing aggregate arrest data, Teplin's work does not examine variability in arrestees' criminal activity, and seems to tell us more about police behavior than it does about the criminality of the mentally ill.

While one may argue that the principal strength of Teplin's observational research lies in its ability to gather information about the full range of arrest incidents involving the mentally ill, ample evidence suggests that the subset of emotionally troubled persons who are most inclined to be criminal are also most inclined to be institutionalized (Monahan & Steadman, 1983). Indeed, the correlates of criminality appear to be the same set of demographic factors mediating state hospital admissions (Lurigio & Lewis, 1987; Monahan & Steadman, 1983). Mental patients should therefore be the primary focus of any study examining the criminality of the mentally disordered. Likewise, from a policy standpoint it makes the most sense to direct our empirical attention toward criminal patients who have been hospitalized: they place the greatest strain on our resources, and they are a clearly identified group that provides us with a tangible target for policy-relevant proposals and interventions.

In summary, previously reported research on crime and mental disorders is deficient in several basic respects. The literature is replete with investigations that rest entirely upon gross comparisons between mental patients and the general population. These studies contribute little to our understanding of individual differences among patients who commit crimes, and they leave a number of critical questions unanswered: e.g., What are the motivations underlying criminal behavior among mental patients? Which patients are most likely to commit serious criminal offenses? What are patients' patterns of movement between the criminal justice and mental health systems? These critical questions are also left unanswered by observational studies, which are based on too few instances of police encounters with the mentally ill to yield reliable conclusions and do not address the prime population of interest in this area, i.e., state mental patients.

In this chapter, we fill existing knowledge gaps by identifying meaningful differences among patients who have committed crimes. Accordingly, the primary purpose of this research is to develop a taxonomy of criminal mental patients from current arrest data, criminal histories, psychiatric records, and patients' self-reports. There are two principal reasons for investigating basic profiles of criminal patients. First, the creation of a taxonomy of the criminal mental patient is a fundamental step toward elucidating the relationship between criminality and mental disorders. A profile delineation will help to explain the varying clinical significance and importance of crime in the lives of different patients.

There is nothing intuitively appealing about the notion that mental patient arrestees comprise a singular or homogeneous category of individuals. After all, the psychiatric nomenclature is testimony to the varied nature of mental disorders (American Psychiatric Association, 1980), and criminologists have generated numerous typologies to describe and explain variability in criminal behavior; these diversities suggest that treating offenders as a monolithic class is a gross oversimplification (Gottfredson & Tonry, 1987). The data reported here call for an extension of that viewpoint to mental patients who partake in crime; they are also consistent with Monahan and Steadman's (1983) assertion that ignoring within-person differences in criminal behavior and mental disorders is tantamount to committing the "ecological fallacy in reverse." Thus, it appears reasonable (almost axiomatic) to posit that mental patients who engage in crime will present differentiable profiles or patterns with respect to such variables as severity and type of offense, degree of criminal intent, criminal and psychiatric histories, hospital utilization, and demographics.

The findings of Lurigio and Lewis (1987) strongly support this proposition. The data reported in that study indicated that while there is a great deal of variability between different patient groups with respect to the seriousness and extent of their criminal and psychiatric histories, there is little variation within a patient group on these dimensions, i.e., similar categories of patients tend to commit the same general types of offenses throughout their careers and are admitted to the hospital at a fairly stable rate. Those results provided the impetus for the present investigation.

Second, the profile delineation will enable us to make more informed decisions about the treatment of criminal mental patients. In the current era of deinstitutionalization, we cannot afford to rely on wholesale observations about mental patient criminality (Bachrach, 1986). It is important to know, in more precise terms, which patients are most likely to jeopardize public safety and how patients' criminal behavior covaries with their mental disorder. Refining ways to identify and categorize criminal mental patients may help mental health practitioners to recognize when and what types of interventions can be effective in helping patients to remain out of trouble with the law and to predict which patients, when released, will pose the greatest threat to the community.

The following discussion relies on data from several sources. For purposes of the current investigation, we examined responses to the following open-ended questions from the interviews with patients: Have you ever been arrested? How many times have you been arrested? What were the charges? Have you ever obtained money in ways that have caused you trouble with the law? Have you been in contact with the police in the past three months (and why)? Have you ever been incarcerated? Where? For how long?

Official Arrests and Criminal Histories. We obtained information from the Chicago Police Department's Bureau of Investigations concerning whether patients in the sample had been arrested within a recent eighteen-month period (July 1985–December 1986). Along with identifying information about patient arrestees, we obtained official police incident reports, which described the nature of the charges leveled against patients, patient demeanor during the episode (e.g., resistive, violent, intoxicated), and any implicit or explicit references to the patients' mental status. In addition, we acquired official criminal histories for all the patients. These furnished a summary of recorded adult criminality, which listed arrests and case dispositions.

Current Admissions and Psychiatric Histories. We obtained current admissions records and psychiatric histories from the state's Department of Mental Health; these included diagnosis at intake and discharge from the hospital, total number of previous admissions, and number of admissions during the months of the study.

We derived a taxonomy of criminal mental patients through a multivariate approach known as cluster analysis, which has been applied successfully in classificatory studies of criminal populations (Brennan, 1987). As a classification procedure, cluster analyses sort cases into groups that are internally homogeneous but maximally different from each other on one or more criteria (Aldenderfer & Blashfield, 1984). This procedure helps us to understand the divergence of classes on several variables simultaneously and is much more powerful than a simple or bivariate cross-classification of data. For example, it creates groups that (a) contain a higher level of information, (b) correspond more closely to the richness and complexity of cases being classified, and (c) have greater predictive, descriptive, and theoretical validity (Brennan, 1987).

Description of the Criminal Sample

We begin with a description of arrests and hospital admissions, criminal and psychiatric histories, and self-reported crime for all the patients in our sample. We report these findings to lend greater clarity and meaning to the three criminal patient groups emerging from our cluster analysis. Then we present the cluster solution.

MENTAL PATIENT CRIMINALITY

Types of Arrests. Nineteen percent (60 out of 313) of the random sample of mental patients were arrested during the eighteen-month period of interest. A total of 128 charges was brought against patients, which arose from 106 separate arrests. The mean number of arrests was 1.77 per arrestee with a standard deviation of .72. Twenty percent (n=26) of the arrests were for felony charges. Only twelve of the arrests (11 percent) were for violent crimes. The charges most commonly brought were criminal damage/trespass to land and disorderly conduct; the least common charges were drug possession and prostitution.

Criminal Histories. The criminal histories of mental patients were more extensive and serious than suggested by their recent arrests, which resulted mostly from misdemeanors and property offenses. Thirty-six percent (n=114) of the random sample of patients, including 75 percent of the arrested patients, had been arrested from 1 to 55 times previously (not including the arrest(s) that transpired during the eighteen months under review). A total of 129 patients had either been recently arrested or possessed a criminal history. The criminal mental patients with prior records had collectively engaged in a total of 978 recorded illegal activities—a mean of approximately nine previous arrests for the group. In contrast to the minor crimes for which patients were recently apprehended, 26 percent (n=260) of patients' past arrests involved alleged violent offenses, e.g., murder, rape, armed robbery, aggravated battery, and aggravated assault. Overall, 36 percent of all the charges cited in their records were for felonies.

Current Hospitalizations. Our analyses of current psychiatric admissions demonstrated that within a twelve-month period, criminal mental patients entered the hospital on 298 separate occasions, a mean of 2.31 hospitalizations per patient. The vast majority of criminal patients (80 percent) were institutionalized voluntarily and were diagnosed as schizophrenic (37 percent) or affective disordered (37 percent). On the average, criminal patients spent approximately four weeks in the hospital during the year we interviewed them.

Psychiatric Histories. Sixty-seven percent of the patients who were arrested for the first time during the investigation (n=10) and 58 percent of the patients with previous criminal records (n=66) also had psychiatric histories, i.e., they had been institutionalized at least once prior to the study's onset. According to state psychiatric records, 42 percent of the criminal patients had been admitted to the mental hospital six or more times in their adult lives.

CHARACTERISTICS OF CRIMINAL PATIENTS

Blacks aged 18–34 were over-represented in the criminal group (i.e., patients with a recent arrest or a prior record (n=129), when compared to their prevalence in the noncriminal group (i.e., patients who had never been arrested, n=184). Age (t (311)=6.70, p<.001) and race (x^2 (2)=16.11, p<.001) differences were both highly significant. Although females constituted 37 percent of the noncriminal patients, they comprised only 15 percent of those who had been arrested (x^2 (1)=34.37, p<.001). Marital status appeared to be marginally related to criminality: among noncriminal patients, the proportion currently married was more than twice that among criminal patients (x^2 (1)=2.87, ns). Criminal and noncriminal mental patients, however, did not differ with respect to their diagnoses (x^2 (4)=5.15, ns), admission status (x^2 (1)=9.23, ns), education (x^2 (4)=1.37, ns), or employment (x^2 (1)=1.02, ns). The majority of patients in both groups were unemployed, had been voluntarily admitted to the hospital, had completed a high school education, and were diagnosed at intake as manifesting either a schizophrenic or affective disorder.

As expected, in our analyses of self-report data we found that a significantly greater proportion of patients with an official criminal record (88 percent) reported that they had been arrested when compared to the proportion of patients (26 percent) reporting arrests in the noncriminal patient sample, i.e., those without any officially recorded arrests (x^2 (1)=51.71, p<.00001). Both criminal and noncriminal patients were most likely to report involvement in a municipal or property offense and least likely to report involvement in a victimless offense. Also, half of the patients in both the criminal and noncriminal groups admitted engaging regularly in income-generating activities (e.g., shoplifting, selling drugs, prostitution) that caused them trouble with the law. Further, criminal and noncriminal patients were equally likely to report drug or alcohol problems, which are frequently associated with criminal behavior.

Finally, our analyses showed that criminal mental patients had a significantly greater number of previous admissions than noncriminal patients, i.e., their psychiatric histories revealed more state hospitalizations than noncriminal patients, holding age constant (x^2 (2)=7.06, p<.03). There was no difference, however, between the two groups on number of current admissions (x^2 (2)=1.54, ns).

Profiles of Criminal Patients

We employed a k-means clustering algorithm to identify criminal mental patients who had different patterns of arrests and psychiatric hospitalizations (Hartigan, 1975). For the purpose of deriving the clusters, we used only those patients who had either a recent arrest or a prior criminal record. The criterion variables we chose for the analysis were number of arrests and admissions during the study, number of lifetime arrests and admissions, and crime seriousness, which measured the overall severity of patients' combined arrests and criminal histories. The crime seriousness index we applied is described by Lurigio (1986). We defined an optimal cluster solution as one that (a) maximized the number of subjects remaining in each cluster, and (b) minimized the off-diagonal elements of the pooled within-cluster matrix of correlations among the five criterion variables (Hartigan, 1975).

Table 8–1. The MHPP Sample: Distinguishable Patterns of Criminal Behavior: Analysis of Variance

Measures	Cluster			F	Newman-Keuls
	1	2	3		
Recent Admissions					
Mean	2.42	1.92	2.56	4.46*	2<1,3
Standard deviation	1.21	.98	1.17		
Prior Admissions					
Mean	5.83	3.36	5.33	10.80**	2<1,3
Standard deviation	2.35	3.23	2.14		
Recent Arrests					
Mean	.96	.56	.88	6.26**	2<1,3
Standard deviation	.36	.75	.54		
Prior Arrests					
Mean	8.13	5.36	9.17	28.27**	2<1,3
Standard deviation	3.24	1.89	2.73		
Crime Seriousness Index					
Mean	1.78	2.63	4.38	3.28*	1<2<3
Standard deviation	2.07	2.15	2.27		

*p<.05
**p<.01

The analysis produced a three-cluster solution. Table 8–1 presents the results of univariate ANOVA on the criterion variables across each of the three clusters. A multivariate test (MANOVA=574.35, p < .001) and all univariate tests of cluster differences were significant. As shown, patients in cluster 1 and cluster 3 were more likely to be arrested and to be hospitalized within the follow-up interval than patients in cluster 2. There were no differences between patients in cluster 1 and cluster 3 as to either recent arrests or hospitalizations. This pattern of results also emerged from the analyses of psychiatric and criminal histories. Again, patients in cluster 1 and in cluster 3 had a greater number of total arrests and hospitalizations than patients in cluster 2. In addition, there was a significant difference between clusters on the crime seriousness index, cluster 3 scores being significantly higher than both cluster 1 and cluster 2 scores, and cluster 2 scores being significantly higher than cluster 1 scores.

The next stage of the analysis tested whether the profiles of arrests and hospitalizations were associated with significant differences on demographics, adjustment, diagnoses, admission status, offense seriousness, size of social network, and self-reported offenses. With respect to demographics, a one-way analysis of variance revealed a significant difference on age, $F(2, 126)=6.06$, $p<.001$. Newman-Keuls tests demonstrated that patients in cluster 3 were significantly younger than patients in clusters 1 and 2, who did not differ on age. Univariate ANOVA on income, amount of public aid, and educational level yielded nonsignificant findings. Also, chi-square tests failed to reveal any significant differences between clusters on race, marital status, and sex.

Analyses on the adjustment measures showed significant differences on mean GAS ratings ($F(2, 125)=14.37$, $p<.001$) and Functioning Scale scores ($F(2, 126)=8.24$, $p<.001$). By pairwise comparisons, cluster 1 patients received lower mean GAS and higher mean functioning ratings than cluster 2 and 3 patients, while cluster 2 patients received lower mean GAS and higher mean functioning ratings than cluster 3 patients. (Higher scores on the functioning scale and lower scores on the GAS indicate poorer adjustment.) No significant differences between clusters were found for admission status, diagnosis, or size of social network.

PROFILE SUMMARY AND INTERPRETATION

We constructed descriptions of the patient profiles by integrating the cluster solution with patients' self-reports of criminal activity and the information cited in police incident narratives and criminal histories. Cluster 1, which consists of 42 percent of the patients with arrests or records, includes those individuals whose involvement in crime is a likely by-product of their illness. Their criminal histories generally specify offenses such as disorderly conduct, criminal trespass to land, or municipal offenses, e.g., disturbing the peace and public intoxication. These patients engage in few activities designed to break the law and spend much of their time residing in and relying on institutions. Criminal behavior is incidental to their mental disorder. Indeed, being symptomatic in public appears to be their only "crime." The patients in this category are much like those described in Teplin's work, i.e., they are arrested primarily because of their public disruptiveness and are the most likely group to be criminalized (Teplin, 1984).

Cluster 2, which consists of 30 percent of the criminal patients, includes those who resort to criminal behavior as an act of survival or desperation. An inspection of their criminal histories shows a number of minor property offenses (e.g., petty theft, shoplifting) and prostitution. These patients commit crimes to supplement meager incomes or welfare support. Criminal activity within this class occurs in spurts, i.e., a high rate of activity within an abbreviated time period followed by contiguous months of no arrests. This suggests that patients in cluster 2 may be resorting to crime during periods of heightened impoverishment or hardship. Their criminal intent is dubious, and it appears unlikely that the patients have truly adopted a criminal lifestyle. Although they are not being criminalized in its strictest interpretation, these patients do not pose a serious, consistent threat to society.

In contrast, cluster 3 patients, representing 28 percent of the profiles, show patterns of arrests for serious crimes that extend over several years. Within this category, patients typically commit crimes that threaten public safety: residential burglary, assault, rape, and robbery. Their criminal histories are indistinguishable from those of "normal" criminals with respect to type of offenses and the frequency and persistence of criminal activity. Patients in cluster 3 are substantially more likely to be sentenced to probation or prison terms, and are also more likely to be involved in substance abuse and drug sales. Their mental disorder seems incidental or secondary to their criminality. In addition, they are the least seriously impaired by their mental illness. Nonetheless, this group places the heaviest burden on both the mental health and criminal justice systems.

Discussion

The overall patient arrest rate reported here is substantially higher than the rates reported in other studies for comparable follow-up periods (Cocozza, Melick, & Steadman, 1978; Lagos, Perlmutter, & Saexinger, 1977). A partial explanation of this result may lie in the characteristics of the cohort, i.e., disproportionately young, black, poor, unemployed, having a prior criminal record, and residing in the predominantly urban setting that served as the catchment area for the institutions from which the sample was drawn. This finding affirms the conclusion that the variables associated with crime in the general population are essentially the same for mental patient populations, and suggests that it may be useful to apply criminological frameworks to study criminal behavior among patient groups (Lurigio & Lewis, 1987). That is, the extensive theories and findings that have been generated from studies of criminality in the general population may be adopted as valuable points of departure for investigations of criminality in mental patient populations.

The present research offers strong initial support for a typology of the criminal mental patient. Clearly, mental patients who engage in criminal activity are not all alike. The categories emerging from this study are sensible, theoretically intriguing, and empirically sound. The population of criminal mental patients encompasses a rather complex collection of individuals for whom criminal behavior has varying personal and clinical significance. The data demonstrate that criminal patients may be clustered into distinct groups that reflect meaningful differences relating to adjustment, crime serious-ness, rates of arrest and admission, and psychiatric histories. As the first investigation of its type, this inquiry underscores the importance of studying crime and mental disorders to yield data that specify the intra-individual and social correlates of offending among diverse groups of patients.

The results of this chapter have interesting implications for the understanding and treatment of mental patients. The three clusters indicate that the problem of criminal behavior among mental pa-tients in the community must be addressed on a variety of fronts. Cluster 1 patients, who are decidedly more annoying than danger-ous, raise the issue of social control and force us to contemplate more appropriate and effective mechanisms for regulating patients' conduct in public places. As did Teplin's (1984) research, this study demonstrates that arresting patients for typical nuisance offenses is quite ineffective as a social control strategy, as shown by the recur-rence of arrests among cluster 1 patients who do not appear to be altering their behavior in response to being taken into police custody.

The characteristics of cluster 2 patients remind us of the powerful linkage between institutionalization and poverty; they suggest that preparing certain categories of patients to be more financially self-sufficient may be a way to divert them from criminal pursuits.

The actions of cluster 3 patients reveal that while mental patients en masse are no more dangerous than members of the general population, members of a particular subgroup present a serious threat to others. These patients can be recognized by their criminal histories and should be screened out of residential treatment centers and segregated from the rest of the institutionalized patient population, who may become the victims of cluster 3 patients while in the hospital (Lurigio & Lewis, 1987).

The current findings highlight the critical need to build better bridges between the criminal justice and mental health systems. In part, this entails the development of strategies for identifying patients who are also criminals and criminals who are also patients. Broader lines of communication and more open dialogue between practitioners in these fields may help to formulate workable and constructive responses to psychiatric patients, who often find their way into jails and prisons, and to criminals, who often find their way into psychiatric institutions. Further, more research is required to understand the confluence of mental disorders and criminality. This chapter is only a beginning effort to develop a classificatory scheme for criminal mental patients. We expect that these findings will spur future replication to test their applicability to other patient populations.

VOLUNTARY COMPLIANCE AND MENTAL HEALTH POLICY

The worlds of the mentally ill are filled with pain and limits. With few resources and little help outside their small circle of friends and family, the mentally ill struggle to find the income and intimacy to make a go of life in civil society. Their illnesses compound an already difficult situation as they struggle for a sense of self-worth and dignity. This combination of disability and poverty seriously impedes progress toward what the rest of us would call a normal life. Within this world, the state hospital is a resource for patient and family alike. It is the place to which they both can turn when troubles appear. For those who cannot develop or have not maintained a network of friends and family, the hospital becomes one of the building blocks of life in this inclusionary system. For those who have such personal support, the state hospital is still there when crises appear.

Although the private sector has generated a variety of services and agencies that care for and treat those who meet their entry and behavioral requirements, these agencies have done little to reduce the state patients' reliance on the hospitals. We could find no evidence beyond medication compliance that these agencies played a role in improving functioning among patients in the community or reducing the number of rehospitalizations among state patients. Indeed, it may be that the state hospitals and the private agencies form a loop from which few patients escape. The public and private sectors supplement each other in caring for those who need mental health services. This situation is not the failure of policy, but rather a consequence of a policy that requires mentally ill persons to live as best they can among us.

Let us be clear about who these people are who build their lives around this state and private sector aid. They are not the sickest of those who seek care. They are not the oldest. These are young males who have not found a place for themselves in the world because of

a complex mix of illnesses, poverty, and the capacities of those around them to handle them and the trouble they bring. Traditional clinical services are not capable of changing them or their circumstances. Indeed, these services seem to have little appreciable effect on the patients' movements and capacities. Given the problems that state mental patients face and the limits of our resources, both economic and clinical, this situation is not likely to change. We must deinstitutionalize our technology so as to care for and control this group.

The changes in mental health policy that we have been concerned about have not been isolated instances. The mental health system was transformed in part by the same forces that have changed other systems that regulate the lives of people. In the world of public education, for example, these changes have created a set of policies that makes segregation by race illegal and unacceptable but does not make integration mandatory (Taylor, 1986). In other words, the government is taking appropriate action in outlawing segregation, but it does not have the authority, as far as most people are concerned, to force integration. This doctrine of *voluntary compliance* lies at the heart of mental health policy as well as educational policy. We now have a system of control and care in which we will not tolerate the exclusion of the mentally ill, but we will not support the forced integration of the mental patient. The extent to which a patient makes a life in the community is not a matter for state coercion. Money, family networks, and patient perceptions all play pivotal roles in the inclusion of the mentally ill in the social worlds we all take for granted. These factors are also pivotal in the utilization of both private and state services. All of these forces are amenable to state action if we expand our thinking and commitment to a fuller life for the disabled.

The time when we could exclude the mentally ill from our social worlds is long past. While some may pine for those days of segregation and isolation, changes in policy, law, and public opinion have made it very unlikely that we will ever return to an exclusionary policy. The transition has not been easy. As patients' mobility has increased, many of our institutions and agencies have had a difficult time adapting to the new constraints that shape the care and management of the mentally ill. Families and friends have had to take more responsibility for the mentally ill, but they have not received any increase in resources or knowledge to cope with these new challenges. The state mental hospitals have been totally transformed in their operation yet still remain the place of first and last resort for both families and other agencies and services who look for help with those who are troubled. Private sector services are available to those who meet their entry and behavioral requirements, but they have become more of a supplement than an alternative to institutional care. Scholars and policy makers have been slow to grasp the nature of the transformation of the mental health system. They continue to battle over who is to blame for the current state of affairs without recognizing the new worlds that have been created for the mentally ill. In these new worlds, patients play a more central role based on how they see their illnesses and the resources they can bring to bear on the problems they face.

The revolution in the care of the mentally ill that has taken place over the last thirty years has changed the relationships between professionals and patients. Just as the "discovery of the asylum" and the Freudian invasion of America changed the way professionals related to the mentally ill, so has the adoption of the inclusionary system. Professionals who spend every day trying to help the mentally ill and their families are well aware of these changes and are beginning to make progress in delivering the kinds of care needed, while recognizing the shifts in power and perception that have occurred.

The relationships between the patient, the professional, and the community are radically different now, and we must build our knowledge base to handle this new situation. Introducing isolated new programs (clinical innovationism) and new diagnostic categories (mental health exceptionalism) will not speed the adoption of new styles of care and control. We must find ways to build on the experiences of practitioners and families in caring for this poor and mobile patient population and make that knowledge the core of the system, rather than the informal adaptations that are made in spite of the system.

The patients who seem to function better in this system are those who learn to define their problems in clinical terms, take their medication, and develop a personal and professional network of people who will accept them for what they are. Some will get better over time, but most will have to live with a chronic disability that will make their lives hard.

The findings of this study suggest that more work with the families of the mentally ill would be very useful, as would more adequate help in staying out of the hospital. Housing seems to be another important area where the state should step in. It also seems clear from this study that a group of patients with the least severe clinical impairment is involved in serious criminal activity. For this group, we need a better criminal justice response, for the current system fails to protect the community. We suggest a coordinated effort with the courts and police to identify these persons and handle their cases through the criminal justice system.

What does it take to build a life? In America, the answer is simple: a job and a family, or other sources of income, support, and intimacy. Without money and human contact, life in civil society is very difficult. Most of us take these two building blocks for granted until we lose one of them. Without money, we cannot purchase the essentials for living in our consumer society, and without intimacy and support, the isolation of city life is very debilitating. Everyone, including the mentally ill, must find income and intimacy to get along in civil society.

No one, of course, starts from scratch. We emerge from childhood with certain connections and resources that give the transition to adulthood meaning and direction. How we relate to others also affects how we use these building blocks from youth. The state mental patient has trouble building a life. If work and family are missing or in disarray, an independent existence will not be a viable alternative to relying on state-sponsored surrogates for income and friendship. The mental health system has not thought of itself as being in the business of supplying income and intimacy. The system has said that the patient is sick first and a member of society second, so that the system ought to supply clinical interventions rather than the necessities of basic support. Accordingly, the mentally ill should get better or be stabilized first; others are responsible for putting their lives back together. The latter task, coming after the clinical intervention has taken place, is the responsibility of the patient and his or her resource network, not the service system.

These assumptions may have been justified in the era when segregation was coterminous with treatment, but when treatment is not exclusionary, mental health exceptionalism and guild innovationism lead to misunderstanding and poor treatment. The patient's life is not put on hold while he is being treated. In all clinical settings, including the state hospital, the patient still maintains his place in the community, trying to make it work as a place to live. The separation of care and normal life makes little sense: care is a part of life and it is assessed by the patient in terms of its capacity to nurture and support him or her. Indeed, the patient treats care as a building block in that life. If that care does not make sense to him or her, one's commitment to it may be very weak.

An inclusionary system fuses the problems of care and living in ways that most policy analysts have yet to address. Treatment does not precede living; treatment is part of living. Treatment for many state mental patients is tied closely to income, food, clothing, and shelter. If money and intimacy are the keys to living in civil society, and these patients have little of them, questions of work and welfare cannot be disentangled from most treatment settings.

Most adults in our society want to earn a living and be independent. We all have been raised to think of our jobs as ways to gain income and prestige. When we cannot work and we cannot secure income, we find our possibilities limited and our standing with ourselves and others lower. State mental patients have very little money and few friends. Most receive some kind of welfare and report very low incomes. Their prospects for funds and friends are limited.

The mental health system in large cities is shaped by these changes. Social and economic policy have often been aimed at bolstering the position of the disabled and poor. The improvements in the lives of the elderly over the last thirty years is a good example of a success. Mental health policy must now move toward supporting the mentally ill more directly. To do less condemns the mentally ill to that world between exclusion and integration where society can neither help nor control those afflicted with serious mental illness.

APPENDIXES
SELECT BIBLIOGRAPHY
INDEX

APPENDIX A
DESCRIPTION OF THE SAMPLING AND
INTERVIEWING PROCEDURES

Goals of the Study

The Mental Health Policy Project (MHPP) was a three-year investigation designed to trace the social and psychological adjustment of Chicago-area mental patients who were admitted to state institutions and then released to the community. The project was funded by a joint grant from the Chicago Community Trust (CCT) and the Illinois Department of Mental Health (DMH).

Sample Selection

The subjects of the study were randomly chosen from the population of Chicago-area mental hospitals from mid-1983 through 1984. A demographic profile—the percentages of patients, categorized by race, sex, age, and number of previous admissions of this population—derived from data provided by the DMH, is presented in table 3–2 in chapter 3. These percentages guided the sample selection for the study and this table shows the percentages from this population selected for this study. The only significant difference between the population of patients in Chicago and the sample selected for this study is in the percentages selected for the number of previous admissions. Our sample was deliberately enriched with subjects who had been repeatedly hospitalized because only 22 percent of the DMH population had been admitted more than five times. If our sample contained such a low proportion of frequent admittees, there might be too few of these people to allow for valid comparisons across the three admission groups.

Beginning in May 1985, magnetic tapes containing information on possible respondents (identified by DMH identification number only) were sent to us on a weekly basis from the central DMH office in Springfield. From these tapes, cases were randomly selected for inclusion in the study.

Choosing the Sample

The weekly tapes we received from DMH revealed that most people who were hospitalized had been previously admitted. This was counter to our expectation that we would have fewer people with hospitalization histories than not and we therefore altered our method of sampling. To ensure that, in our model population, the proportion of patients with no previous admissions would approximate the proportion (41 percent) in the total DMH population, we drew samples from 100 percent of the patients not previously admitted and 50 percent of those previously admitted. For those people who were previously admitted, we stratified the sample on age, assuring that the full range of ages in the population would be represented in the sample.

For those cases where a sampling fraction was used, we designed a stratified random sample, stratifying explicitly on number of previous admissions and implicitly on facility (choosing only those hospitals that served Chicago residents) and age of patient. The cases were sorted so that all facilities and the full range of ages would be well represented.

The following outlines the procedures used by programmers to select the weekly sample.

1. Only those cases from hospitals serving Chicago residents were included in the sample: Tinley Park Mental Health Center, Illinois State Psychiatric Institute (ISPI), Chicago-Read Mental Health Center, and Madden Mental Health Center. Furthermore, only those cases who would be released to Chicago and the Chicago area would be sampled. These cases included those people from Chicago and in the regions of North Chicago, South Chicago, and suburban Cook County.

2. Three subfiles were created based on people with no previous admissions, one to five previous admissions, and six or more previous admissions.

3. Each subfile was sorted by facility and age.

4. All people with no hospitalization history and half of those with at least one previous admission were selected for the sample.

5. A random sort procedure on the cases was performed and frequencies were run each week on the sample in order to verify that residence and age were within the properly specified ranges of the sample design.

Our target number of completed interviews was 350, but we specified from 375 to 575 interviews to be completed to account for incomplete interviews. On July 19, 1985, we began to sample from our weekly hospital tapes.

Interviewing the Sample

LOCATING PATIENTS IN THE HOSPITAL

A listing of the target patients' identification numbers, admission dates, admitting regions, hospitals, and units, in addition to necessary demographic information (age, race, and sex) was distributed to our interviewers each week. Interviewers were to select interviewees by order of identification number on their printouts, but interview only those people who were soon to be released from the hospital (within one to two weeks). In actuality, patients were interviewed typically by unit and then by identification number. This was especially true at facilities where units were in separate buildings and it was inconvenient for interviewers to travel from one unit to another to look for a specific person. Interviewers relied upon the unit head's knowledge about the patient's discharge date to determine whether the patient was soon to be released. Fourteen patients who were expected to be released from the hospital within one to two weeks of the first interview were still in the hospital six months later when contacted for the second interview.

Patients were paid $10 for their participation in the study. Participation included completing the Life Events Interview and being diagnosed according to the Schedule for Affective Disorders and Schizophrenia (SADS) (Endicott & Spitzer, 1978) by a clinician not associated with the hospital. In addition, patients had to agree to be reinterviewed for the study at two later dates.

It took several days for the DMH to copy its weekly patient popula-

Table A–1. The MHPP Sample: Reasons for Attrition

Type of Attrition	Number
Prior to Contact	
Patient discharge	851
Subsequent to Contact	
Patient refusals	99
Symptom interference	92
Transfers or chronic patients	103
Incomplete interviews	8
Total	302
Total	1,153

tion onto tape and mail it to us. It took another day or two to randomize the patient identification numbers and distribute them to the interviewers. Almost one week may have passed before interviewers arrived on the hospital units to seek out interviewees. Owing to this delay, many potential interviewees were released before interviewers could contact them. Most of those released had no prior hospitalization history.

Our staff kept a record of their contacts. Tallies made of the number of patients who had been discharged, had refused to be interviewed, were unavailable for interview (in restraints, assessed as dangerous to the welfare of the interviewer), or transferred, indicate that the overwhelming majority of potential patients lost from our sample were discharged prior to contact (table A–1). Because many of the patients with no previous admissions history were discharged before our interviewers were able to contact them, we anticipated that the sample would weigh heavily toward severely disturbed patients. This was expected because hospital staff routinely discharge first-time admittees with acute problems more quickly than chronic patients in an effort to reintegrate them into the community. In addition, interviewers reported that many first-time admittees refused to be associated with any study on mental illness. Of 1,466 people we attempted to locate, 58 percent had already been discharged at the time of attempted contact, 7 percent refused to be interviewed, 6 percent were assessed as too dangerous to the interviewer to be interviewed, and 7 percent had been transferred to another hospital or were not expected to leave the hospital soon.

To counterbalance the biasing effect of the quick release of non-chronic patients on our sample, we decided to select persons at the hospital with high patient identification numbers, indicating that the patient had experienced no previous psychiatric hospitalizations. Of the thirty-one people chosen in this way, twenty (65 percent) had no prior admissions, nine (29 percent) had been hospitalized fewer than six times, and two (6 percent) had at least six prior admissions. This selection procedure compensated for the large potential loss of patients through hospital discharge prior to contact.

A second concern for our staff was that, after several weeks, the number of people listed on the weekly tapes diminished and interviewers were not completing the number of interviews originally anticipated for them. A call to the DMH revealed that some days at the ends of eight weeks had been left off the tapes. Over the two-month period, twelve days, nine of which were Fridays, had been omitted. The patient admissions for these days were submitted via a separate tape, but since weeks had passed before these omissions were discovered, most of the people admitted on those days had already been discharged from the hospital.

Of the 321 interviews partially or totally completed by patients, eight were eliminated from the study because less than one-third of the interview was completed. The final number of completed interviews used in our study is 313.

SAMPLE CHARACTERISTICS

As with the eighteen-month, 1983–84 DMH population, two-thirds of our sample are between ages 18 and 34 with Chicago-Read having more people aged 35 and over than the other facilities. Our ratio of men to women is also about 6:4, although we have a slightly higher percentage of men in our sample (63 percent) than does the DMH population (61 percent). The racial makeup of our sample is almost identical to that of the DMH population for all hospitals except ISPI. At ISPI, we interviewed more blacks and fewer Hispanics than are representative of the total DMH population. The overall demographic composition of our sample, however, is much the same as the 1983–84 DMH population. The greatest sampling variability between the MHPP and the DMH derives from the undersampling of people with fewer than six previous admissions and the oversampling of chronic mental patients.

Table 3–2 in chapter 3 also compares our total sample of 313 patients with the total DMH population for 1983–84. Our sample percentages for sex, race, and age are almost identical to the percentages in the total DMH population for that period. There were, however, significant differences in patient hospitalization history. These differences are due to our contacting people who were available at the hospital, i.e., those people who had been kept long enough for interviewers to reach them. Thus, our expectation of sampling bias on the basis of chronicity was well-grounded.

INDEPENDENT DIAGNOSIS OF PATIENTS

After the Life Events Interview was completed, the interviewer submitted the name and identification number of the interviewee to an independent clinician, who was to administer the SADS to each patient. These clinicians had been trained by a two-person team affiliated with a private hospital in Chicago. Clinicians diagnosed patients on the SADS either the day of the interview, or the next day, although some patients were released before clinicians could contact them. Of the 313 patients for whom we have complete information on the Life Events Interview, we have independent diagnoses on the SADS for 204. Eighty-eight percent of the ISPI sample, 75 percent of both the Madden Mental Health Center and the Chicago-Read samples, but only 37 percent of the Tinley Park sample was diagnosed via SADS administration.

The close proximity of ISPI to the hospital where the clinicians were based and the great distance between this base and the other hospitals, especially Tinley Park, accounts for much of the attrition between completed interviews in the hospital and completed diagnoses on the SADS.

FOLLOW-UP PROCEDURES: FINDING PATIENTS IN THE COMMUNITY

The interviews in the hospital began in July 1985 and ended in October 1985. While interviewers were still in the field, we began follow-up procedures for the second interview in the community, pursuing a variety of avenues to locate participants. About thirty days prior to the interview, we attempted to trace former patients and their significant others by letter, notifying them to expect our call to arrange an interview date. We traced these persons through the addresses and phone numbers the respondents provided in the first interview.

In our letters to patients, we underscored the importance of their continued participation and reminded them that they would be paid $10. Letters to significant others were designed to uncover any information regarding recent changes in the patient's phone number and/or residence. Within approximately thirty days after the mailings, interviewers attempted to contact patients and significant others by phone. To increase the likelihood of achieving a contact, calls were made on various days; we set a limit of ten calls per person. The names of patients and significant others whose letters were returned and who could not be reached by phone were sent to the U.S. Post Office for forwarding information. Individuals whose letters were not returned were mailed a second notification letter. During this process, we often called Directory Assistance and the Reverse Directory Service; we also consulted Commonwealth Edison's Listing of Residences in order to verify and obtain valid phone numbers and addresses. Another important aspect of our follow-up procedures was the ongoing inspection of DMH hospital records to determine whether any of the patients who had not been found through the preceding means were currently psychiatric inpatients or residing in community-based shelters or residential treatment centers. A special DMH data tape that contained information about patients' use of aftercare and residential treatment was also accessed. Aftercare agencies were contacted by letter and/or phone regarding the whereabouts of participants. In addition, we queried the Cook County Department of Corrections to identify any patients who were presently incarcerated.

THE COMMUNITY INTERVIEW

Three forms of the second interview were developed. Most people (n=187) were in the community at the time of the second interview and received the Life Events Interview (Form C1). This interview focused on community activities and also asked about any hospitalizations between the initial interview and this second interview in the community. It also included the SADSC (Endicott & Spitzer,

Table A–2. The MHPP Sample: Results of Wave 2 Follow-up Attempts, January 1986–July 11, 1986 (N=313)

Disposition of Interview	N	%
Completed Interviews	210	67
Non-Completions	103	33
Unable to locate patient	47	15
Patient refused	32	10
Patient moved out of Chicago area	18	6
Patient deceased	6	2
Total	313	100

1978), which assesses any changes in diagnosis and overall functioning of the person in the community. Two other forms of the Life Events Interview were developed for fourteen people who had never left the hospital and nine who spent some time in the community but were in the hospital at the time of the second interview.

SAMPLE CHARACTERISTICS OF FORMER PATIENTS IN THE COMMUNITY

Table A–2 presents the results of our follow-up attempts to locate former patients in the community. A total of 210 (67 percent) of the initial sample was interviewed in the community. Only 47 (15 percent) of the original 313 respondents could not be located. Seventy-nine percent of the contacted patients agreed to be reinterviewed. Twenty-three of the participants were in the hospital, and three were incarcerated at the time the second interview was conducted. The most common reason for attrition was the patient's refusal to be reinterviewed. In some cases, it was the patient's family that prohibited the interview.

WAVE 3 OF THE STUDY

For the third and last phase of the study, we selected two subsamples to be reinterviewed. One group comprised people whom we could not locate or who refused to be interviewed at the second wave. A

Table A–3. The MHPP Sample: Demographics and Prior Admissions by Admitting Facility, Wave 2 Respondents (N=210)

	Read %	Read N	Madden %	Madden N	Tinley %	Tinley N	ISPI %	ISPI N
Sex								
Male	67	62	61	27	66	29	59	17
Female	33	31	39	17	34	15	41	12
Race								
Black	34	32	61	27	84	37	79	23
White	57	53	34	15	7	3	14	4
Hispanic	8	7	2	1	5	2	3	1
Other	1	1	2	1	5	2	3	1
Age								
18–34	61	57	73	32	73	32	72	21
35–49	31	29	14	6	18	8	14	4
50–65	8	7	14	6	9	4	14	4
Previous Admissions								
0	29	27	30	13	25	11	45	13
1–5	31	29	3	17	27	12	31	9
6+	40	37	32	14	48	21	24	7
% of Total (N)	44	93	21	44	21	44	14	29

second group consisted of people who had been readmitted to the hospital since their second interview and had been diagnosed with the SADS by the independent clinical team. One hundred thirty-two people were targeted for interviews in the third wave of the study. Of this target sample, fifteen people who had previously refused to be interviewed, or whom we were unable to locate at the second wave, were interviewed a second time, and forty-two people who had been hospitalized since the second interview, and also had a SADS diagnosis, were interviewed a third time.

Table A–3 displays the number of completed interviews for people in the community by the hospital where their first interview was completed. Slightly more patients from Read and Madden and slightly fewer patients from Tinley Park were reinterviewed in the community than in the hospital. Comparisons of the base and follow-

Table A–4. The MHPP Sample: Comparing Wave 1 and Wave 2 Samples

	Wave 1 Respondents (N=313) %	Wave 2 Respondents (N=210) %	Statistical Test For Differences
Sex			
Male	64	64	χ^2 (1)=0, ns
Female	36	36	
Race			
Black	56	57	χ^2 (2)=.894, ns
White	34	36	
Other	10	7	
Age			
18–34	66	68	χ^2 (2)=.153, ns
35–49	23	22	
50–65	11	10	
Previous Admissions			
0	36	30	χ^2 (2)=2.29, ns
1–5	32	32	
6+	32	38	

up samples as to demographics and previous admissions disclosed no significant differences. However, an apparent trend in the data suggests that chronic patients (i.e., those with six or more prior hospitalizations) were more likely to be reinterviewed than first-time admittees (table A–4).

Coding of Interviews

A team of coders was hired to transform the data in the interviews into computer-readable form. Many of the responses in the Life Events Interview could be recorded as a number on a coding sheet. Responses to open-ended questions had to be redefined in numerical form. A codebook was prepared, in which each item on the interview was transformed into a variable with column designation, field specification, and possible codes, for use by the coders. Problems in interpretation of information and other coding issues were discussed and resolved at weekly meetings with the project coordinator.

Responses obtained in the interviews in the hospital and the community were coded over a one-year period. A subset of them then was recoded to assess reliability. All codesheets were then sent to a private keypunch facility to be entered onto tape. We then defined the taped data on SPSS system files for our analyses.

Reliability coefficients (values of Cronbach's alpha) indicate that coding accuracy is a function of the range of codes available for each variable and the difficulty in interpreting each question. Responses to narrowly focused questions such as "Where were you born?" or "What is your present religion, if any?" were coded with high reliability by the coders. Responses to either/or questions, such as "Have you ever been arrested?" also were reliably coded. Reliabilities were lower for responses that had a large range of codes and were subject to coders' judgments. For example, the reliability among coders for coding the question, "Can you think of any two things, again no matter how big or small, that have made you feel unhappy during the past two weeks?" was .71 for the first mention and .32 for the second mention.

Conclusion

The procedures employed by the MHPP yielded a sample of hospitalized patients that closely approximated the total DMH state population. Our painstaking efforts to contact patients for the second stage of our investigation were quite successful. Nearly 70 percent completion in a panel design with mental patients is clearly superior to the response rates that are commonly reported in similar kinds of studies. While our base sample of patients overrepresents chronic admittees, there is no systematic bias between our patient sample and our sample of people in the community.

Appendix B

Life Events Interview

Basic Questionnaire Used for First Interview

"Hello, my name is _____ and I'm from Northwestern University. I am part of a research team that is interviewing people who have been treated in state hospitals to find out how they feel about their lives and how they help themselves in times of trouble. You have been selected by chance to participate in this study. Because I am taking up your time with our questions, I will pay you $10. By answering the questions in this interview, you will help me get information on how people manage their lives.

Some questions are personal, and you are free to stop the interview whenever you wish. I very much want to know how you feel and I hope that you can spend the time talking with me. Your answers will be kept confidential and your name will not be used in any reports that we write. Your cooperation will be greatly appreciated.

This paper will be the only thing which has your name and it will be kept separate from anything you tell me throughout the interview.

This interview will probably take more than one hour. Do you have the time now to answer some questions?"

| IF NO: | "When would be more convenient to set up a meeting time?"

(ASK ONLY IF APPLIES)

| IF YES: | "I need your written consent that you are voluntarily answering the questions I am about to ask. Would you please read this paper and sign your name to it?"

I.D. ____ ____ ____ ____ ____ ____

What is your full name? _____

(DETACH THIS SHEET FROM QUESTIONNAIRE)

I.D. ____ ____ ____ ____ ____ ____

NAME OF INTERVIEWER _____

PLACE OF INTERVIEW _____
(NAME OF PLACE & ADDRESS)

_____

DATE _____ STARTING TIME _____

DAY OF WEEK _____

SEX OF RESPONDENT:
MALE..0
FEMALE...1

First, I'd like to ask you some short questions about your background.

1. Where were you born?
CHICAGO...1
SUBURBS OF CHICAGO.........................2

_____
(SPECIFY NAME OF SUBURB)
OTHER ILLINOIS.....................................3

_____
(SPECIFY NAME OF TOWN)
OTHER UNITED STATES 4
NON-UNITED STATES.............................5
DON'T KNOW...8
NO ANSWER 9

2. How many years have you lived in the Chicago area? _____
DON'T KNOW ....-8
NO ANSWER...-9

3a. Where will you stay when you leave the hospital?
WITH PARENTS...1
WITH SPOUSE...2
WITH FRIEND IN HIS/HER HOME..............3
OWN APARTMENT..4
HOTEL/YMCA...5
NURSING HOME..6
INTERMEDIATE CARE; SHELTER CARE...7
OTHER _____ 8
(specify)
DON'T KNOW...9 (GO TO Q6)

3b. What is the name of the _____?
(Use Person's Term)

4. What is the address of this place?

_____

5a. Is this the same place you lived before you went to the hospital?
      YES ....1 (GO TO Q6)
      NO...0 ⎤
                                                             ⎥

      5b. "How is it that you will be staying in a different ⎦
           place?"   ⟵

           _____

           _____

           _____

6. In the last 6 months, how many times have you changed your residence?

_____

7. On the average, how much do you worry about whether you will have a place to stay when you leave the hospital? Would you say you worry. . .
      A GREAT DEAL 4
      SOMEWHAT 3
      A LITTLE, or..2
      NOT AT ALL? 1
      DK 8
      REFUSED 9

8. Some people prefer to stay in the hospital while others would rather stay outside the hospital. Which do you prefer?
      IN HOSPITAL 1
      OUTSIDE HOSPITAL 2
      DK 8
      REFUSED 9

    COMMENTS _____

_____

_____

9. How would you describe yourself in terms of ethnic background? (PROBE: What country does your family come from?)
(WRITE IN ALL RESPONSES GIVEN BY S)

_____

_____

_____

10. What language do you speak most often?
      ENGLISH 1
      SPANISH 2
      OTHER _____ 3
                   (specify)

11a. What is your present religion, if any?

    PROTESTANT..1
    CATHOLIC..2
    JEWISH...3
    NONE..4
    OTHER _____ 5
                          (specify)

    11b. What specific denomination is that?

    BAPTIST 1
    METHODIST...2
    LUTHERAN 3
    PRESBYTERIAN 4
    EPISCOPALIAN 5
    OTHER _____ 6
                          (specify)
    NON-APPLICABLE.................................0

12. What race do you consider yourself?

    BLACK...1
    WHITE...2
    HISPANIC 3
    ASIAN 4
    OTHER _____ 5
                          (specify)
    DON'T KNOW...8
    REFUSED TO ANSWER 9

13. What is the year of your birth? _____

14. What was your last year of school completed?

    _____
    (CONVERT ANSWER TO EXACT NO. OF YEARS)

15. What was the last year of school your father completed?

    _____
    (CONVERT ANSWER TO EXACT NO. OF YEARS)

16. What was the last year of school your mother completed?

    _____
    (CONVERT ANSWER TO EXACT NO. OF YEARS)

EDUCATION CODE

1 2 3 4 5 6 7 8	9 10 11 12	13 14 15 16	17 18
ELEMENTARY SCHOOL	HIGH SCHOOL	COLLEGE	M.A. +

(PROBE FOR EXACT NUMBER OF YEARS AND/OR TYPE OF DEGREE)

17. Up to the time you were 16 years old, whom did you live with most of the time?

> BOTH PARENTS 1
> MOTHER..2
> FATHER 3
> GRANDPARENT..4
> OTHER RELATION 5
> FOSTER PARENTS.....................................6
> LIVED IN AN INSTITUTION 7
> SOMEONE ELSE _____ 8
>   (specify)
> REFUSED TO ANSWER 9

18. While you were growing up, did anyone in your family, not including yourself, live in an institution like a nursing home or hospital or prison?

> YES 1
> NO..0 (GO TO Q19)

Tell me about that.

(PROBE FOR CATEGORY OF PERSON, E.G., SISTER, PARENT)
(PROBE FOR TYPE OF INSTITUTION, ESPECIALLY WHETHER MENTAL HOSPITAL)

_____

_____

_____

_____

_____

19. Is your father living?

> YES 1
> NO..0
> DON'T KNOW...8
> REFUSED TO ANSWER 9

20. What does (did) your father do for a living? What is (was) his job? IF RETIRED, ASK What did he do for a living?

(WRITE ALL ANSWERS GIVEN. PROBE FOR SPECIFIC JOB)

_____

_____

_____

_____

21. What was your mother's usual occupation while you were growing up? (WRITE DOWN ALL RESPONSES)

_____

_____

_____

_____

22. Have you ever been married?

    YES ....1 (GO TO Q23)

    NO..0 (GO to Q26)

23. How many times? _____

    REFUSED TO ANSWER 9

24. Are you . . .

    CURRENTLY MARRIED...........................1 (GO TO Q25)

    SEPARATED 2

    DIVORCED, or...3

    WIDOWED?...4

    REFUSED ....9 (GO TO Q26)

25. How many years have you been married? _____ (GO TO Q28a)

26. Before you came to the hospital did you live alone or with someone?

    ALONE...0 (GO TO Q28a)

    WITH SOMEONE ....1 (GO TO Q27)

    REFUSED...9

27. Was this a . . .

    LOVER..1

    FRIEND..2

    ADULT RELATIVE(S)..............................3

    CHILD, or..4

    SOMEONE ELSE _____ 5
                    (specify)

    REFUSED 9

28a. Do you have children?

    YES 1

    NO..0 (GO TO Q29)

    DON'T KNOW...8

    28b. How many children do you have? _____

         DON'T KNOW....................................-8

         REFUSED TO ANSWER.................-9

What is the sex and age of each child?

28c.		Sex	28d.	Age
	Male	Female		
	0	1		
1)	0	1		_____
2)	0	1		_____
3)	0	1		_____
4)	0	1		_____
5)	0	1		_____
6)	0	1		_____

29. Now I'd like to talk to you about your life now.

Can you think of any two things, no matter how big or small, that have made you feel good during the *past two weeks* . . . anything that comes to mind?

IF YES:

1) _____

_____

_____

_____

2) _____

_____

_____

_____

No ____0____

30. Can you think of any two things, again no matter how big or small, that have made you feel unhappy during the past two weeks?

IF YES:

1) _____

_____

_____

_____

2) _____

_____

_____

_____

No ____0____

31. Can you think of one thing you'd like to change in your life . . . something that would make your life better?

    IF YES:

    1) _____

    _____

    _____

    _____

    No _____ 0 _____

32. Now let's talk about some of the things you do with your time. Which of the things I read have you done during the past week?

    I'm going to read each item and ask you to respond yes, or no.

	YES	NO
Gone for a walk	1	0
Gone to a movie or play	1	0
Watched TV	1	0
Gone shopping	1	0
Gone to a restaurant or coffee shop	1	0
Gone to a bar	1	0
Read a book, magazine or newspaper	1	0
Listened to a radio	1	0
Played cards or games	1	0
Gone for a ride in a bus or car, or the "el"	1	0
Prepared a meal	1	0
Worked on a hobby	1	0
Gone to a sports activity	1	0
Played a sport	1	0
Gone to a meeting for some organization or social group	1	0
Gone to a park or zoo	1	0
Gone to a library	1	0
Worked around the house or garden	1	0
Just sat and thought	1	0
Took a class at a school	1	0
Gone to a party	1	0
Did volunteer work	1	0
Gone to a community center	1	0
Gone to a laundromat	1	0
Gone to a religious service	1	0
Telephoned and just talked with a member of your immediate family	1	0
Telephoned and just talked to a more distant relative	1	0
Got together with a member of your immediate family	1	0
Got together with a more distant relative	1	0

Telephoned and just talked to a close friend
outside the hospital ....1.......0
Telephoned and just talked to an acquaintance
outside the hospital ....1.......0
Got together with a close friend ....1.......0
Got together with an acquaintance ....1.......0

Please look at this. (HAND SUBJECT THE DELIGHTED-TERRIBLE SCALE.) This is called the Delighted-Terrible Scale. Can you read it OK, or would you like some help?

During the interview we'll be using this scale to help you tell me how you feel about different things in your life. All you have to do is tell me what on the scale best describes how you feel. For example, if you were someone who loves chocolate ice cream, you might point to "delighted." On the other hand, if you hate chocolate ice cream, you might point to "terrible." If you feel about equally satisfied and dissatisfied with chocolate ice cream, then you would point to the middle of the scale.

Do you have any questions about the scale?

I'm going to ask you some more questions about what you do with your time now.

33. A. How do you feel about the way you spend your spare time? (USE ONLY FOR CLARIFICATION: Your free time.) Would you say you feel . . .

DELIGHTED, ...7
PLEASED, ...6
MOSTLY SATISFIED, ...5
MIXED, ...4
MOSTLY DISSATISFIED, ...3
UNHAPPY, or 2
TERRIBLE 1
DON'T KNOW 8
REFUSED 9

B. How do you feel about the amount of time you have to do the things you want to do? Would you say you feel . . .

DELIGHTED, ...7
PLEASED, ...6
MOSTLY SATISFIED, ...5
MIXED, ...4
MOSTLY DISSATISFIED, ...3
UNHAPPY, or 2
TERRIBLE 1
DK 8
REFUSED 9

C. How do you feel about the chance you have to enjoy pleasant or beautiful things? Would you say you feel . . .

    DELIGHTED, ...7
    PLEASED, ...6
    MOSTLY SATISFIED, ...5
    MIXED, ...4
    MOSTLY DISSATISFIED, ...3
    UNHAPPY, or 2
    TERRIBLE 1
    DK 8
    REFUSED 9

D. How do you feel about the amount of fun you have? Would you say you feel . . .

    DELIGHTED, ...7
    PLEASED, ...6
    MOSTLY SATISFIED, ...5
    MIXED, ...4
    MOSTLY DISSATISFIED, ...3
    UNHAPPY, or 2
    TERRIBLE 1
    DK 8
    REFUSED 9

E. How do you feel about the amount of relaxation in your life? Would you say you feel . . .

    DELIGHTED, ...7
    PLEASED, ...6
    MOSTLY SATISFIED, ...5
    MIXED, ...4
    MOSTLY DISSATISFIED, ...3
    UNHAPPY, or 2
    TERRIBLE 1
    DK 8
    REFUSED 9

F. How do you feel about the pleasure you get from the TV or radio? Would you say you feel . . .

    DELIGHTED, ...7
    PLEASED, ...6
    MOSLTY SATISFIED, ...5
    MIXED, ...4
    MOSTLY DISSATISFIED, ...3
    UNHAPPY, or 2
    TERRIBLE 1
    DK 8
    REFUSED 9

G. Could you tell me how you feel about your standard of living—your food, housing, medical care, furniture, recreation and things like that? Would you say that you feel . . .

DELIGHTED, ...7
PLEASED, ...6
MOSTLY SATISFIED, ...5
MIXED, ...4
MOSTLY DISSATISFIED, ...3
UNHAPPY, or 2
TERRIBLE 1
REFUSED 8
DK 9

H. How do you feel about your life now as a whole? Would you say that you feel . . .

DELIGHTED, ...7
PLEASED, ...6
MOSTLY SATISFIED, ...5
MIXED, ...4
MOSTLY DISSATISFIED, ...3
UNHAPPY, or 2
TERRIBLE 1
DK 8
REFUSED 9

34. Now I will hand you some cards. Please sort this deck of cards into two piles. One pile represents "like me now." (PLACE "LIKE ME NOW" CARD IN FRONT OF INTERVIEWEE.) The second pile is "not like me now." (PLACE "NOT LIKE ME NOW" CARD NEXT TO OTHER CARD.) I will read a card and hand it to you. Please place each card *under* the appropriate card, either "like me now" or "not like me now."

		Like me now	Not like me now
(0)	I FREQUENTLY GIVE *ADVICE* TO OTHERS	1	0
(+2)	I AM AN *AFFECTIONATE* AND UNDERSTANDING PERSON	1	0
(0)	I *AGREE* WITH WHAT EVERYONE SAYS	1	0
(−1)	I FREQUENTLY GET *ANGRY* WITH OTHER PEOPLE	1	0
(+1)	I WILL *ARGUE* BACK WHEN I FEEL I AM RIGHT ABOUT SOMETHING	1	0
(−1)	I WILL *BELIEVE* ANYONE	1	0
(−2)	I CAN BE A *COLD* AND UNFEELING PERSON	1	0
(−1)	I AM A *COMPETITIVE* PERSON	1	0
(+1)	WHEN NECESSARY, I CAN *COMPLAIN* ABOUT THINGS THAT BOTHER ME	1	0
(+2)	I AM *CONSIDERATE* OF OTHERS	1	0
(+2)	I AM A *COOPERATIVE* PERSON	1	0

(+1)	GENERALLY I CAN BE *COUNTED ON* TO HELP OTHERS...............1............0	
(0)	I AM *CRITICAL* OF OTHER PEOPLE...................1............0	
(+1)	I AM ABLE TO *CRITICIZE* AND FIND FAULT WITH MYSELF ....1............0	
(0)	I AM FREQUENTLY *DISAPPOINTED* BY OTHER PEOPLE ....1............0	
(−2)	I AM SOMEWHAT OF A *DOMINATING* OR BOSSY PERSON........................1............0	
(−1)	I AM EASILY *EMBARRASSED*.............................1............0	
(+2)	I AM *FIRM* BUT FAIR IN MY RELATIONS WITH OTHER PEOPLE..........................1............0	
(+2)	I AM *FRANK* AND HONEST WITH PEOPLE.........1............0	
(+2)	I AM A *FRIENDLY* PERSON............................1............0	
(−1)	USUALLY I *GIVE IN* WITHOUT TOO MUCH OF A FUSS.................................1............0	
(+1)	I AM *GRATEFUL* FOR WHAT OTHER PEOPLE DO FOR ME ....1............0	
(0)	I AM OFTEN *HELPED BY* OTHER PEOPLE..........1............0	
(+1)	I BELIEVE THAT I AM AN *IMPORTANT* PERSON.................................1............0	
(+1)	I ENJOY BEING *IN CHARGE* OF THINGS ....1............0	
(+1)	I AM AN *INDEPENDENT* AND SELF-CONFIDENT PERSON.......................1............0	
(+2)	I AM A GOOD *LEADER*...............................1............0	
(−1)	I AM TOO *LENIENT* WITH OTHER PEOPLE ....1............0	
(+1)	I *LOVE* EVERYONE ....1............0	
(0)	I WANT EVERYONE TO *LOVE ME*.......................1............0	
(−1)	I PREFER TO LET OTHER PEOPLE *MAKE DECISIONS* FOR ME ....1............0	
(+1)	I CAN BE *OBEDIENT* WHEN NECESSARY...........1............0	
(0)	I AM *PROUD* AND SELF-SATISFIED ....1............0	
(−2)	AT TIMES I ACT *REBELLIOUS* OR FEEL BITTER ABOUT SOMETHING...........................1............0	
(+1)	I CAN *REPROACH* PEOPLE WHEN NECESSARY ...1............0	
(+2)	I AM A *SELF-RESPECTING* PERSON ....1............0	
(−1)	I AM *SHORT-TEMPERED* AND IMPATIENT WITH MISTAKES OTHER PEOPLE MAKE ....1............0	
(+2)	I *SPOIL* PEOPLE WITH KINDNESS ....1............0	
(+2)	I AM ABLE TO *TAKE CARE* OF MYSELF ....1............0	
(+1)	I OFTEN *TAKE CARE* OF *OTHER* PEOPLE ....1............0	
(0)	I HARDLY EVER *TALK BACK* ....1............0	
(+1)	I AM SOMEWHAT *TENDER* AND SOFT-HEARTED........................1............0	
(+2)	PEOPLE *THINK WELL* OF ME ....1............0	
(−1)	I AM RATHER *TIMID* AND SHY ....1............0	
(−2)	I AM *TOUCHY* AND EASILY HURT BY OTHERS .1............0	
(−2)	IT IS HARD FOR ME TO *TRUST* ANYONE ....1............0	

(+2)   I AM A *TRUSTING* PERSON ....1............0
(−2)   FREQUENTLY I FEEL *WEAK* OR HELPLESS......1............0

35. Now I would like you to rate yourself on how you think you manage your life. Let's start with money management . . .

In terms of managing your money, do you feel that you . . .

DON'T NEED ANY HELP.........................1
NEED SOME HELP...................................2
NEED A LOT OF HELP 3
DK..8
REFUSED 9

36. Apart from whether you are presently employed or want to be, do you feel you . . .

ARE READY TO BE EMPLOYED.............1
(FULL-TIME OR PART-TIME)
ARE READY TO BE EMPLOYED IN
A SHELTERED WORKSHOP.................2*
ARE NOT READY TO BE EMPLOYED....3
DK..8
REFUSED 9

*IF ASKS: WHAT IS A SHELTERED WORKSHOP? SAY:
A work program or activity run by a community center that will pay you less than the minimum wage for the work you do.

37. In terms of taking care of basic needs like keeping clean and dressing appropriately, do you feel you . . .

DON'T NEED ANY HELP.........................1
NEED SOME HELP...................................2
NEED A LOT OF HELP 3
DK..8
REFUSED 9

38. With your household chores, such as laundry, cleaning, and cooking, do you feel you . . .

DON'T NEED ANY HELP.........................1
NEED SOME HELP...................................2
NEED A LOT OF HELP 3
DK..8
REFUSED 9

39. To get public transportation, do grocery shopping, or get services you need, do you feel that you . . .

DON'T NEED ANY HELP.........................1
NEED SOME HELP...................................2
NEED A LOT OF HELP 3
DK..8
REFUSED 9

40. Now, I'd like you to rate yourself as to how you manage with other people.

Do you feel that the way you act with people is OK . . .
IN MOST SOCIAL SITUATIONS..............1
IN SOME SOCIAL SITUATIONS.............2
IN VERY FEW SOCIAL SITUATIONS.....3
DK...8
REFUSED 9

41. Do you feel that in meeting your responsibilities to other people, you . . .
DON'T NEED ANY HELP.........................1
NEED SOME HELP...................................2
NEED A LOT OF HELP 3
DK...8
REFUSED 9

42. Do you show feelings appropriately . . .
IN MOST SOCIAL SITUATIONS..............1
IN SOME SOCIAL SITUATIONS.............2
IN VERY FEW SOCIAL SITUATIONS.....3
DK...8
REFUSED 9

43. Do you feel that you can find activities to do in your free time . . .
ON YOUR OWN...1
WITH SOME HELP....................................2
WITH A LOT OF HELP..............................3
DK...8
REFUSED 9

44. In getting aftercare services* do you feel that you . . .
DON'T NEED ANY HELP.........................1
NEED SOME HELP...................................2
NEED A LOT OF HELP 3
DK...8
REFUSED 9
*[AFTERCARE SERVICE: An agency that helps you to cope with life after the hospital.]

45a. Now I'd like to ask you about the mental hospital. In the few weeks before you came to the hospital, did you have housing problems?
YES 1
NO...0
DK 8

45b. Tell me about them?   ←

46a. Did you have money problems?

        YES 1

        NO..0

        DK 8

    46b. Tell me about them?   ←

47a. Did you have family problems?

        YES 1

        NO..0

        DK 8

    47b. Tell me about them?   ←

48a. Did you have emotional problems?

        YES 1

        NO..0

        DK 8

    48b. Tell me about them?   ←

49a. Did you have problems with alcohol or recreational drugs?

        YES 1

        NO..0

        DK 8

    49b. Tell me about them?   ←

50a. Did you have problems in taking prescribed medication?

        YES 1
        NO...0
        DK 8

    50b. Tell me about them.   ←

_____

_____

_____

51. Please tell me how you came to be admitted to the mental hospital the last time. (FOLLOW-UP PROBES)
    a. What were the events that occurred twenty-four hours before you entered the hospital that led you to the hospital? Let's talk about that day.
    b. Who recommended that you go to the hospital for help? (self, family member, friend, police, agency. . .) Who took you to the hospital?
    c. Did you agree with _____ that you should go to the hospital or did you oppose going to the hospital, at first?
    d. What was said or done that convinced you to go the hospital, i.e., what are the reasons people gave you that led you to enter the hospital?

_____

_____

_____

_____

_____

_____

_____

_____

_____

_____

_____

_____

_____

_____

_____

_____
_____
_____
_____
_____
_____
_____
_____
_____
_____
_____
_____
_____
_____
_____
_____
_____
_____
_____
_____
_____
_____
_____

52. Did you . . .
    a. behave in ways that were unusual or embarrassing?
    b. behave in ways that made people afraid of you, i.e., did you hit or threaten anyone that day?

> IF YES:
> DID RESPONDENT HIT OR THREATEN TO HURT?
> YES 1
> NO..0
>
> WERE POLICE INVOLVED?
>
> YES 1
> NO..0

COMMENTS: _____

_____
_____
_____
_____
_____
_____
_____
_____
_____
_____
_____

53. What was the most important cause of your hospitalization?

_____
_____
_____
_____
_____
_____
_____
_____
_____
_____

54. Now I'd like to find out about your problem and how it affects you.
   What do you call the problem that you have? (PROBE: What name does it have?) (IF CLAIMS HAS NO PROBLEM, GO TO Q66)

_____
_____
_____

55. What do you think has caused your problem? (PROBE: How did you get it?)

_____

_____
_____
_____
_____
_____

56. Why do you think it started when it did? (PROBE: Do you feel that you were born with this problem? Did something start the problem?)

_____
_____
_____
_____
_____
_____
_____

57. What does your _____ do to you—how does it work?
    Use Persons' Term (UPT)

(PROBE: How does it affect you, e.g. your ability to work, think clearly, or your relationships with other people?)

_____
_____
_____
_____
_____
_____
_____
_____
_____
_____
_____
_____

58. How severe is it? (PROBE: Do you think that other people have _____ worse than you do?)
    <u>UPT</u>

_____

_____

_____

59. Will it have a long or short course? (PROBE: Will it last forever?)

_____

_____

_____

60. What do you fear most about _____?
    <u>UPT</u>

_____

_____

_____

_____

_____

_____

61. What are the chief problems _____ has caused for you?
    <u>UPT</u>

_____

_____

_____

_____

_____

_____

_____

62. What treatment do you think you should receive?

_____

_____

_____

63. What are the most important results you hope to receive from the treatment?

_____

_____

_____

_____

64. In what way has _____ affected your relationship with your family? (PROBE: parents, siblings, children, spouse)

_____

_____

_____

_____

65. What do the people in the hospital call your problem?

_____

_____

_____

_____

66. What type of treatment are you receiving in the hospital now?

_____

_____

_____

67. What is your official diagnosis? _____

68. In the two months before you entered the hospital, were you seeing anyone for treatment or counseling or going to a self-help group?

YES ....
NO..0 (GO TO Q69)

a. Who did you see? ←

	1st mention	2nd mention
MEDICAL DOCTOR	1	1
PSYCHIATRIST	2	2
OTHER MENTAL HEALTH PROFESSIONAL	3	3
CLERGY	4	4
SELF-HELP GROUP	5	5
OTHER _____ specify	6	6
DON'T KNOW	8	8

b. Where did you see these people?

        1st mention   2nd mention

_____   _____

     (name of place & address)

c. In the two months prior to your hospitalization, how often did you see _____ ?

                                  (UPT)

                            1st mention   2nd mention

	1st mention	2nd mention
FEW TIMES A WEEK	5	5
1/WEEK	4	4
1/2 WEEKS	3	3
1/MONTH	2	2
LESS THAN 1/MONTH	1	1
DON'T KNOW	8	8
REFUSED	9	9

d. Each time you saw _____, about how much time did you spend with him (her/them)?

        1st mention   2nd mention

_____   _____

        (minutes)   (minutes)

e. Describe the type of treatment you received. (PROBE FOR TYPE OF TREATMENT: GROUP, INDIVIDUAL, FAMILY, RECREATIONAL, VOCATIONAL)

    1st mention _____

_____

    2nd mention _____

_____

f. What part of the treatment did you find most helpful, if any?

    1st mention _____

_____

    2nd mention _____

_____

g. Did you get help with practical problems also, such as housing or money problems? (IF YES, PROBE FOR DETAILS)

    1st mention _____

_____

2nd mention _____

_____

_____

h. Before you came to the hospital this last time, did you try to get help from _____ ?
(UPT)

1st mention

YES 1
NO...0

2nd mention

YES 1
NO...0

i. How is it that you (did not get) got help? What happened?

1st mention _____

_____

2nd mention _____

_____

_____

69a. Were you ever a patient in a psychiatric ward or hospital before this last time?
YES 1
NO..0 (GO TO Q70)

b. During the past year, how many times were you hospitalized? _____

c. How many times have you been hospitalized altogether? _____

d. How long was the hospitalization the time before this one?

_____ months   _____ years.

(CONVERT TO DAYS) _____

e. The first time you were admitted to a psychiatric hospital, how old were you?

_____ years.

f. What were the names of all the hospitals you were ever admitted to for treatment?

_____

_____

_____

_____

_____

70a. When you entered the mental hospital this last time, was it officially a voluntary or involuntary hospitalization?

VOLUNTARY 1

INVOLUNTARY...2

70b. Did you want to go to the hospital?

YES 1

NO..0

DK..8

70c. COMMENTS _____

_____

_____

_____

71a. What medications, if any, are you now taking? (IF NONE: GO TO Q78)

1. _____

2. _____

3. _____

4. _____

5. _____

6. _____

7. _____

8. _____

9. _____

71b. IF LITHIUM: Have you had your lithium blood levels monitored?

YES 1

NO..0 (GO TO Q72)

71c. How often are they monitored?

_____

72. How often do you take . . .

	1st	2nd	3rd	4th	5th
1/DAY	1	1	1	1	1
2/DAY	2	2	2	2	2
3/DAY	3	3	3	3	3
4/DAY	4	4	4	4	4
MORE THAN 4/DAY	5	5	5	5	5
DON'T KNOW	8	8	8	8	8

73. How much do you take of _____ each time? _____
    1st mention

    (PROBE: ASK IF THEY KNOW NO. OF MILLIGRAMS)

    _____ each time? _____
    2nd mention

    _____ each time?_____
    3rd mention

    _____ each time?_____
    4th mention

    _____ each time?_____
    5th mention

74. Do you have trouble remembering to take the medication?
    YES 1
    NO...0 (GO TO Q75)

    Sometimes it's hard to take medication. Would you say
    you actually take it . . .   ←
    ALMOST ALL THE TIME 3
    SOMETIMES..2
    NOT VERY OFTEN....................................1
    DON'T KNOW 8
    REFUSED 9

75a. Do you get side effects from the medication?
    YES 1
    NO...0 (GO TO Q76)

    75b. What side effects do you get from the medication?   ←

    _____

    _____

    _____

    _____

    75c. What side effects are you most worried about
    getting from the medication?

    _____

_____

_____

_____

75d. Do you have any long-term side effects that concern you?

_____

_____

_____

76. Do you feel it is important to you to take these medications, or doesn't
it matter much whether you take them or not?

IMPORTANT...1

NOT IMPORTANT....................................0

77a. Have you ever stopped taking these medications even though a doctor
said you should keep taking them?

YES ....1 ⎤

NO...0 (GO TO Q78)

77b. Why? (PROBE: Chose not to take medications,
forgot?) ←⎦

_____

_____

_____

77c. What happened after you stopped taking the
medication?

_____

_____

_____

78. Do you drink alcoholic beverages?

YES .... ⎤

NO...0 ⎦

How often do you drink alcoholic beverages? ←

EVERY DAY OR ALMOST EVERY DAY............4

A FEW TIMES A WEEK....................................3

WEEKENDS ONLY, or..2

SOCIALLY, AT PARTIES OR ON A DATE........1

REFUSED..9

79. Now I'd like to know about some of your plans after the hospital.

    Do you plan to go to any social service agencies or people for help after you leave the hospital?

    YES 1

    NO..0 (GO TO Q84)

80. What agencies or people? (PROBE: Anywhere else?)

    1st MENTION _____

    2nd MENTION _____

    3rd MENTION _____

81. Have you been there before?

	1st Mention	2nd Mention	3rd Mention
YES	1	1	1
NO	0	0	0

82. Have you had contact with them since you've been in the hospital to discuss your life after the hospital?

	1st Mention	2nd Mention	3rd Mention
YES	1	1	1
NO	0	0	0

83. Did the hospital assign you to this agency?

	1st Mention	2nd Mention	3rd Mention
YES	0	0	0
NO	X	X	X
	↓	↓	↓

    How did you hear about it? _____ ↵

    1. _____

    2. _____

    3. _____

84. Now, I am going to mention some types of problems that people can have.

    Please tell me the first person or organization you went to for help the last time you had a . . . (WRITE IN RESPONDENT'S ANSWER. IF GIVES NAME, PROBE FOR ROLE: BROTHER, FRIEND, ETC.)

    (PROBE: IF PROFESSIONAL IS MENTIONED, ASK, Is this person with an agency?)

    a. money problem _____

    _____

    b. housing problem _____

    _____

c. job problem _____

_____

d. health problem _____

_____

e. personal problem _____

_____

85. Imagine you felt yourself getting upset or feeling bad. Do you know some organization or person that you would go to for help?

NO...0 (SKIP TO Q86)
YES 1
DK..8 (SKIP TO Q86)
REFUSED ....9 (SKIP TO Q86)

| IF YES: | What person or organization would you go to? (CIRCLE ALL THAT APPLY. PROBE: Anywhere else?) |

	1st Mention	2nd Mention	3rd Mention
PERSON:			
MOTHER/FATHER	1	1	1
BROTHER/SISTER	2	2	2
AUNT/UNCLE	3	3	3
SON/DAUGHTER	4	4	4
GRANDPARENT	5	5	5
GRANDCHILD	6	6	6
OTHER RELATIVE	7	7	7
FRIEND	8	8	8
NEIGHBOR	9	9	9
MEDICAL DOCTOR	10	10	10
MENTAL HEALTH PROFESSIONAL	11	11	11
CLERGY	12	12	12
OTHER (_____)13			
_____	13	13	13
ORGANIZATION: CHURCH OR TEMPLE	14	14	14
COMMUNITY MENTAL HEALTH AGENCY	15	15	15
MENTAL HOSPITAL	16	16	16
OTHER HOSPITAL	17	17	17
SELF-HELP GROUP	18	18	18
HALFWAY HOUSE	19	19	19
OTHER AGENCY _____	20	20	20
DK	-8	-8	-8
REFUSED	-9	-9	-9

How did you first meet (_____NAME_____) ⤆
1st mention
    MENTAL HEALTH-RELATED 1
    NON MENTAL HEALTH-RELATED 0

How did you first meet (_____NAME_____)
2nd mention
    MENTAL HEALTH-RELATED 1
    NON MENTAL HEALTH-RELATED 0

How did you first meet (_____NAME_____)
3rd mention
    MENTAL HEALTH-RELATED 1
    NON MENTAL HEALTH-RELATED 0

86. The next series of questions asks about your relationships with people with whom you discuss important personal matters or with whom you spend time.

Looking back over the last six months, who are the people *with whom you discussed any important personal matter*? Please just give me their first name and last initial. (PUT NAMES ON NAME CARD. AFTER INTERVIEW, ENTER NAMES HERE)

1st Mention _____

2nd Mention _____

3rd Mention _____

4th Mention _____

5th Mention _____
(WRITE DOWN ALL MENTIONS AFTER 5 IN MARGIN BUT DO NOT ASK LATER.)

87a. I just asked you about the people you talk to about important personal matters. What about the people with whom you do things, like have a meal or spend your spare time? Are those. . .
the same people, ...1 (PUT #'S FROM FIRST GRID IN SECOND GRID, GO TO Q89)

different people, ...2
or do you usually spend your time
by yourself? 3
Even so, are there *any* people with whom you spend time? ⤆
    YES 1
    NO ....0 (GO TO Q88b)
What are their names? (PUT NAMES ON NAME CARD, THEN GO TO Q88a). AFTER INTERVIEW, ENTER NAMES HERE. ⤆

87b. 6th Mention _____

7th Mention _____

8th Mention _____

9th Mention _____

10th Mention _____

88a. Where do you and _____#6_____ usually spend time? _____
   (PROBE FOR SETTING, E.G., COFFEE SHOP, LOBBY, ETC., FOR
   EACH PERSON MENTIONED, THEN GO TO Q89)

6th Mention _____

7th Mention _____

8th Mention _____

9th Mention _____

10th Mention _____

88b. Where do you usually spend your time? _____

88c. Are there any important people in your life?
   (IF NO, GO TO Q96.)
   (IF YES, NOTE THEM AND ASK Q89.)

_____

_____

_____

89. I'd like to find out a little about each of these people. (1st name) is
   (male/female)? INSERT YOUR BEST GUESS BASED ON NAME.
   WAIT FOR CONFIRMATION OR CORRECTION FROM RESPON-
   DENT. REPEAT FOR EACH NAME. IF 6-10 IS REPEAT OF 1-5, DO
   NOT ASK.)

	1	2	3	4	5	6	7	8	9	10
Male	0	0	0	0	0	0	0	0	0	0
Female	1	1	1	1	1	1	1	1	1	1

spouse or spouse equivalent: your wife, your husband, or a person with
   whom you are living as if married
boyfriend / girlfriend: someone with whom you go out on formal
   occasions; someone you date
child: your son or daughter
other relative: grandparent, grandchild, cousin, aunt, uncle, nephew,
   niece, in-law
friend: someone with whom you get together for informal social
   occasions such as lunch, dinner, parties, drinks, movies, or visiting
   one another's home

co-worker: someone you work with or usually meet while working
co-group member: member of a group to which you belong—for
    example, someone who attends your church, or whose children
    attend the same school as your children, or who belongs to the same
    club or class in school
professional adviser or consultant: a trained expert you turn to for
    advice—for example, a lawyer
neighbor: someone outside your own household who lives close to you

---

90. Some people can be connected to you in more than one way. For example, a man could be your brother and he could belong to your church and be your lawyer. Please tell me in what ways (lst name) is connected to you.

REPEAT FOR EACH NAME: How is (NAME) connected with you? (INITIAL PROBE: Other ways?—SUBSEQUENT PROBES AS NEEDED: Any other ways?

	1	2	3	4	5	6	7	8	9	10
SPOUSE OR SPOUSE EQUIVALENT	1	1	1	1	1	1	1	1	1	1
BOYFRIEND/ GIRLFRIEND	2	2	2	2	2	2	2	2	2	2
MOTHER	3	3	3	3	3	3	3	3	3	3
FATHER	4	4	4	4	4	4	4	4	4	4
BROTHER	5	5	5	5	5	5	5	5	5	5
SISTER	6	6	6	6	6	6	6	6	6	6
YOUR CHILD	7	7	7	7	7	7	7	7	7	7
OTHER CHILD	8	8	8	8	8	8	8	8	8	8
OTHER RELATIVE	9	9	9	9	9	9	9	9	9	9
FRIEND	10	10	10	10	10	10	10	10	10	10
CO-WORKER	11	11	11	11	11	11	11	11	11	11
CO-GROUP MEMBER	12	12	12	12	12	12	12	12	12	12

    SPECIFY GROUP (_____)

	1	2	3	4	5	6	7	8	9	10
SOCIAL WORKER/PSYCHOLOGIST/ PSYCHIATRIST	13	13	13	13	13	13	13	13	13	13
PSYCHIATRIC NURSE	14	14	14	14	14	14	14	14	14	14
MEDICAL OR FAMILY DOCTOR	15	15	15	15	15	15	15	15	15	15
PROFESSIONAL ADVISOR (OTHER THAN MENTAL HEALTH)	16	16	16	16	16	16	16	16	16	16
CLERGY	17	17	17	17	17	17	17	17	17	17
NEIGHBOR	18	18	18	18	18	18	18	18	18	18
OTHER (_____)	19	19	19	19	19	19	19	19	19	19
DON'T KNOW	-8	-8	-8	-8	-8	-8	-8	-8	-8	-8

91. How long have you known _____?
    (REPEAT FOR EACH PERSON)

	1	2	3	4	5	6	7	8	9	10
LESS THAN 6 MONTHS	1	1	1	1	1	1	1	1	1	1
6-11 MONTHS	2	2	2	2	2	2	2	2	2	2
1-3 YEARS	3	3	3	3	3	3	3	3	3	3
4-6 YEARS	4	4	4	4	4	4	4	4	4	4
MORE THAN SIX YEARS	5	5	5	5	5	5	5	5	5	5
DON'T KNOW	8	8	8	8	8	8	8	8	8	8

92. Where did you first meet _____?
    (REPEAT FOR EACH PERSON)

	1	2	3	4	5	6	7	8	9	10
Mental Health Service Related	1	1	1	1	1	1	1	1	1	1
Non-Mental Health Service Related	0	0	0	0	0	0	0	0	0	0

93. On the average, do you speak with _____
    (REPEAT FOR EACH PERSON) more than once a week, once a week, once a month, or less than once a month?

	1	2	3	4	5	6	7	8	9	10
MORE THAN ONCE A WEEK	1	1	1	1	1	1	1	1	1	1
ONCE A WEEK OR 3 TIMES/MONTH	2	2	2	2	2	2	2	2	2	2
MONTHLY OR LESS THAN 3 TIMES/MONTH	3	3	3	3	3	3	3	3	3	3
LESS THAN MONTHLY	4	4	4	4	4	4	4	4	4	4
DON'T KNOW	8	8	8	8	8	8	8	8	8	8

94. Of all the people we've been talking about, which one would you say has the most influence on you? (CIRCLE #)

1	2	3	4	5	6	7	8	9	10

95. I'd like to know how _____(MOST INFLUENTIAL_____ acts toward you. How much does _____(MOST INFLUENTIAL)_____ . .
    (IF NO ONE IS MOST INFLUENTIAL, ASK FOR FIRST MENTION)

	A GREAT DEAL	SOME-WHAT	NOT AT ALL	DON'T KNOW	RE-FUSED
1. listen to your concerns?	3	2	1	8	9
2. dislike you?	1	2	3	8	9
3. understand you?	3	2	1	8	9
4. resent you?	1	2	3	8	9

 5. care about you?.................................3..........2..........1..........8..........9
 6. have high expectations of you? ....3..........2..........1..........8..........9
 7. have concern for you?.......................3..........2..........1..........8..........9
 8. have confidence in you? ....3..........2..........1..........8..........9
 9. give you helpful advice? ....3..........2..........1..........8..........9
10. like to do things with you?...............3..........2..........1..........8..........9
11. consider things that are most
    important to you?............................3..........2..........1..........8..........9
12. like to have you around?...................3..........2..........1..........8..........9
13. act cold, aloof or nasty to you? ....1..........2..........3..........8..........9
14. respect you? ....3..........2..........1..........8..........9
15. criticize you in a way you
    don't like?.......................................1..........2..........3..........8..........9
16. disapprove of you?...........................1..........2..........3..........8..........9
17. comfort you?....................................3..........2..........1..........8..........9
18. reject you?.......................................1..........2..........3..........8..........9
19. trust you? ....3..........2..........1..........8..........9
20. value your opinions? ....3..........2..........1..........8..........9
21. get angry with you when it's not
    your fault?.......................................1..........2..........3..........8..........9
22. help you with your emotional
    problems?...3..........2..........1..........8..........9
23. show dissatisfaction with you? ....1..........2..........3..........8..........9
24. stand up for you? ....3..........2..........1..........8..........9
25. help you solve money problems?.....3..........2..........1..........8..........9
26. help you with errands if needed? ....3..........2..........1..........8..........9
27. have a depressing outlook or make
    you feel down?................................1..........2..........3..........8..........9
28. help you get to places? ....3..........2..........1..........8..........9
29. help you with everyday chores
    when needed?...................................3..........2..........1..........8..........9
30. give you advice that is not helpful?.1..........2..........3..........8..........9
31. like you the way you are?.................3..........2..........1..........8..........9
32. boss you around? ....1..........2..........3..........8..........9

96. The next items relate to the work that you did in the two months before
    you came to the hospital.

    Were you employed outside the home?
                    YES ....1 (GO TO Q97)
                    NO..0 (GO TO A)

        A. IF NO: Are you a . . .
            HOMEMAKER?* 1
            STUDENT?...2
            RETIRED? 3
            LOOKING FOR WORK?......................................4
            UNEMPLOYED, NOT SEEKING WORK?.........5

VOLUNTEER?...6
OTHER? (specify) ——————————— 7
NA..0
DON'T KNOW...8
REFUSED...9
(* HOMEMAKER: A PERSON WHO TAKES PRIMARY
   CARE OF ANOTHER PERSON)

B. Have you ever been employed?
    YES..................................1 (GO TO C)
    NO ....0 (GO TO APPRO-
                            PRIATE SECTION)

IF VOLUNTEER, GO TO Q97
IF STUDENT, GO TO Q100
IF UNEMPLOYED, GO TO Q101
IF HOMEMAKER, GO TO Q102

C. How long has it been since you have been employed?
                      _____ months
                      _____ years

97. What kind of work do (did) you do? _____
                              RESPONDENT'S ANSWER
(IF *EMPLOYED* NOW, GO TO Q98)
(IF PRESENTLY *NOT EMPLOYED* NOW, GO TO APPROPRIATE
SECTION)

IF VOLUNTEER, GO TO Q97
IF STUDENT, GO TO Q100
IF UNEMPLOYED, GO TO Q101
IF HOMEMAKER, GO TO Q102
IF RETIRED, GO TO Q101

98. How long have you been at this present job? _____ months
                                          _____ years

99. IF EMPLOYED OR VOLUNTEER:

We are going to use the delighted-terrible scale again. (HAND PERSON
D-T SCALE)

A. How do you feel about your job? Would you say you feel . . .
    DELIGHTED,...7
    PLEASED, ...6
    MOSTLY SATISFIED,..............................5

MIXED, ...4
MOSTLY DISSATISFIED, ...3
UNHAPPY, or 2
TERRIBLE 1
DON'T KNOW 8
REFUSED 9
NA 0

B. How do you feel about the people you work with? Would you say
you feel . . .

DELIGHTED, ...7
PLEASED, ...6
MOSTLY SATISFIED, ...5
MIXED, ...4
MOSTLY DISSATISFIED, ...3
UNHAPPY, or 2
TERRIBLE 1
DON'T KNOW 8
REFUSED 9
NA 0

C. How do you feel about where you work . . . the physical surroundings? Would you say you feel . . .

DELIGHTED, ...7
PLEASED, ...6
MOSTLY SATISFIED, ...5
MIXED, ...4
MOSTLY DISSATISFIED, ...3
UNHAPPY, or 2
TERRIBLE 1
DON'T KNOW 8
REFUSED 9
NA 0

D. How do you feel about the number of hours you work? Would you
say you feel . . .

DELIGHTED, ...7
PLEASED, ...6
MOSTLY SATISFIED, ...5
MIXED, ...4
MOSTLY DISSATISFIED, ...3
UNHAPPY, or 2
TERRIBLE 1
DON'T KNOW 8
REFUSED 9
NA 0

E. How do you feel about the amount you get paid? Would you say you feel . . .

DELIGHTED,..7
PLEASED, ...6
MOSTLY SATISFIED,................................5
MIXED,..4
MOSTLY DISSATISFIED,..........................3
UNHAPPY, or..2
TERRIBLE...1
DON'T KNOW..8
REFUSED 9
NA...0

IF STUDENT:

100. A. Are you going to school?

Full-time?...1
Part-time?...2
Taking one class? 3
NA...0

We are going to use the delighted-terrible scale again. (HAND PER-SON D-T SCALE.)

B. How do you feel about being a student? Would you say you feel . . .

DELIGHTED,..7
PLEASED, ...6
MOSTLY SATISFIED,................................5
MIXED,..4
MOSTLY DISSATISFIED,..........................3
UNHAPPY, or..2
TERRIBLE...1
DON'T KNOW..8
REFUSED 9
NA...0

C. How do you feel about your education? Would you say you feel . . .

DELIGHTED,..7
PLEASED, ...6
MOSTLY SATISFIED, ...5
MIXED,..4
MOSTLY DISSATISFIED,..........................3
UNHAPPY, or..2
TERRIBLE...1
DON'T KNOW..8
REFUSED 9
NA...0

D. How do you feel about your school? Would you say you feel . . .

DELIGHTED,..7
PLEASED, ...6
MOSTLY SATISFIED,..............................5
MIXED,..4
MOSTLY DISSATISFIED,.........................3
UNHAPPY, or..2
TERRIBLE...1
DON'T KNOW..8
REFUSED 9
NA...0

E. How do you feel about the other students in your school? Would
you say you feel . . .

DELIGHTED,..7
PLEASED, ...6
MOSTLY SATISFIED,..............................5
MIXED,..4
MOSTLY DISSATISFIED,.........................3
UNHAPPY, or..2
TERRIBLE...1
DON'T KNOW..8
REFUSED 9
NA...0

F. How do you feel about your teachers? Would you say you feel . . .

DELIGHTED,..7
PLEASED, ...6
MOSTLY SATISFIED,..............................5
MIXED,..4
MOSTLY DISSATISFIED,.........................3
UNHAPPY, or..2
TERRIBLE...1
DON'T KNOW..8
REFUSED 9
NA...0

G. How do you feel about your performance in school during the past
year? Would you say you feel . . .

DELIGHTED,..7
PLEASED, ...6
MOSTLY SATISFIED,..............................5
MIXED,..4
MOSTLY DISSATISFIED,.........................3
UNHAPPY, or..2
TERRIBLE...1
DON'T KNOW..8
REFUSED 9
NA...0

IF UNEMPLOYED OR RETIRED:

We are going to use the delighted-terrible scale again. (HAND PER-SON D-T SCALE.)

101. A. How do you feel about not working, given your present life . . . I mean the amount of money you have or the way you live? Would you say you feel . . .

DELIGHTED,...7
PLEASED, ...6
MOSTLY SATISFIED, ...5
MIXED,...4
MOSTLY DISSATISFIED,...........................3
UNHAPPY, or..2
TERRIBLE..1
DON'T KNOW..8
REFUSED 9
NA...0

B. How do you feel about the lack of work in your life? Would you say you feel . . .

DELIGHTED,...7
PLEASED, ...6
MOSTLY SATISFIED, ...5
MIXED,...4
MOSTLY DISSATISFIED,...........................3
UNHAPPY, or..2
TERRIBLE..1
DON'T KNOW..8
REFUSED 9
NA...0

C. (IF RETIRED, GO TO Q103) How do you feel about being unem-ployed? Would you say you feel . . .

DELIGHTED,...7
PLEASED, ...6
MOSTLY SATISFIED, ...5
MIXED,...4
MOSTLY DISSATISFIED,...........................3
UNHAPPY, or..2
TERRIBLE..1
DON'T KNOW..8
REFUSED 9
NA...0

IF HOMEMAKER:

102. We are going to use the delighted-terrible scale again. (HAND PER-
SON D-T SCALE.)

A. How do you feel about being a homemaker? Would you say you
feel . . .

DELIGHTED,...7
PLEASED, ...6
MOSTLY SATISFIED,...............................5
MIXED,...4
MOSTLY DISSATISFIED,.........................3
UNHAPPY, or..2
TERRIBLE...1
DON'T KNOW..8
REFUSED 9
NA...0

B. How do you feel about the number of hours you work? Would you
say you feel . . .

DELIGHTED,...7
PLEASED, ...6
MOSTLY SATISFIED,...............................5
MIXED,...4
MOSTLY DISSATISFIED,.........................3
UNHAPPY, or..2
TERRIBLE...1
DON'T KNOW..8
REFUSED 9
NA...0

C. How do you feel about your performance as a homemaker during
the past year? Would you say you feel . . .

DELIGHTED,...7
PLEASED, ...6
MOSTLY SATISFIED,...............................5
MIXED,...4
MOSTLY DISSATISFIED,.........................3
UNHAPPY, or..2
TERRIBLE...1
DON'T KNOW..8
REFUSED 9
NA...0

FOR EVERYONE:

103. Now I want to ask you some questions about money matters.

Where does the money come from to pay the bills? (CIRCLE ALL
THAT APPLY. READ EACH ITEM.) Your. . .

	YES	NO	NA	DON'T KNOW	RE-FUSED	
Job............................	1	0	7	8	9	ASK ONLY
Spouse's job..............	1	0	7	8	9	IF APPLIES
Family/friends..........	1	0	7	8	9	
Public assistance	1	0	7	8	9	
Anything I haven't mentioned?	1	0	7	8	9	
(specify) _____						

104. How much money do you receive each month from all sources before taxes?

_____

105. A lot of people have irregular jobs or do other things to make ends meet, like panhandling, selling blood, or selling drugs. Do you do anything like this on the side?

        NO..0 (GO TO Q109)
        YES..
        DK...8
        REFUSED...9

105a. Tell me what it is.   ←

_____

_____

_____

106. Has this ever caused you trouble with the law?

        NO..0 (GO TO Q107)
        YES..

        Tell me about it.   ←

_____

_____

_____

_____

_____

107. Altogether about how much money would you say you earned in this way last month? $ _____ (BEFORE HOSPITALIZATION)

        REFUSED ....-888
        DK...-999

108. Did you include this amount earlier when we talked about income from other sources?

INCLUDED..1
ADDITIONAL..2
DK...8
REFUSED..9

HAND PERSON AGREE/DISAGREE SCALE

Next I will read a series of attitude statements. Each represents a commonly held opinion. There are no right or wrong answers. You will probably agree with some items or disagree with others. We are interested in the extent to which you agree or disagree with such matters of opinion. When I read each statement tell me the number which best represents your opinion.

	DISAGREE			AGREE		
	STRONGLY DISAGREE	DISAGREE SOMEWHAT	SLIGHTLY DISAGREE	SLIGHTLY AGREE	AGREE SOMEWHAT	STRONGLY AGREE
109. Whether or not I get to be a leader depends mostly on my ability.	1	2	3	5	6	7
110. To a great extent my life is controlled by accidental happenings.	1	2	3	5	6	7
111. I feel like what happens in my life is mostly determined by powerful people.	1	2	3	5	6	7
112. Whether or not I get into a car accident depends mostly on how good a driver I am.	1	2	3	5	6	7
113. When I make plans, I am almost certain to make them work.	1	2	3	5	6	7
114. Often there is no chance of protecting my personal interests from bad luck happenings.	1	2	3	5	6	7
115. When I get what I want, it's usually because I'm lucky.	1	2	3	5	6	7
116. Although I might have good ability, I will not be given leadership responsibility without appealing to those in positions of power.	1	2	3	5	6	7
117. How many friends I have depends on how nice a person I am.	1	2	3	5	6	7

118. I have often found that what is going to happen will happen.
    1   2   3   5   6   7

119. My life is chiefly controlled by powerful others.
    1   2   3   5   6   7

120. Whether or not I get into a car accident is mostly a matter of luck.
    1   2   3   5   6   7

121. People like myself have very little chance of protecting our personal interests when they conflict with those of strong pressure groups.
    1   2   3   5   6   7

122. It's not always wise for me to plan too far ahead because many things turn out to be a matter of good or bad fortune.
    1   2   3   5   6   7

123. Getting what I want requires pleasing those people above me.
    1   2   3   5   6   7

124. Whether or not I get to be a leader depends on whether I'm lucky enough to be in the right place at the right time.
    1   2   3   5   6   7

125. If important people were to decide they didn't like me, I probably wouldn't make many friends.
    1   2   3   5   6   7

126. I can pretty much determine what will happen in my life.
    1   2   3   5   6   7

127. I am usually able to protect my personal interests.
    1   2   3   5   6   7

128. Whether or not I get into a car accident depends mostly on the other driver.
    1   2   3   5   6   7

129. When I get what I want, it's usually because I worked hard for it.
    1   2   3   5   6   7

130. In order to have my   1   2   3   5   6   7
plans work, I make
sure that they fit in
with the desires of
people who have power
over me.

131. My life is determined   1   2   3   5   6   7
by my own actions.

132. It's chiefly a matter of   1   2   3   5   6   7
fate whether or not I
have a few friends or
many friends.

133. People have different ways of showing irritation or expressing anger.
Have you had any fights with people in the last year in which someone
was physically hurt?

         YES...1
         NO...2 (GO TO Q134)

Please tell me about it . . .   ←

Where did it happen? _____

_____

Who was involved? _____

_____

How did it end? _____

_____

_____

_____

_____

134. In the past three months, tell me when you have had to call a police-
man, talk to the police, or been in any contact with the police. (EACH
TIME, where, when, what happened.)

_____

_____

_____

_____

_____

_____

_____

135. Have you ever been arrested?
  YES...
  NO...00 (GO TO Q137)

  a. How many times? _____ ⟵

  b. What were the charges? _____
  _____

136. Have you ever gone to jail?
  YES...
  NO...000 (GO TO Q137)
  a. Where? _____ ⟵

  b. For how long? _____

137. Now, I'm going to read some statements and I would like you to tell me if they are true or not true about you.

		TRUE	NOT TRUE
A.	I lose my temper easily, but get over it quickly.	1	0
B.	I am always patient with others.	0	1
C.	I am irritated a great deal more than people are aware of.	1	0
D.	It makes my blood boil to have somebody make fun of me.	1	0
E.	If someone doesn't treat me right, I don't let it annoy me.	0	1
F.	Sometimes people bother me just by being around.	1	0
G.	I often feel like a powder keg ready to explode.	1	0
H.	I sometimes carry a chip on my shoulder.	1	0
I.	I can't help being a little rude to people I don't like.	1	0
J.	I don't let a lot of unimportant things irritate me.	0	1
K.	Lately, I have been kind of grouchy.	1	0

138. Have you ever been robbed?
  YES 1
  NO...0

139. Have you ever been physically assaulted on the street?
  YES 1
  NO...0

140. What do you look forward to in the coming years?

_____

_____

_____

_____

_____

_____

_____

_____

_____

_____

_____

_____

141. What concerns do you have for the future?

_____

_____

_____

_____

_____

_____

_____

_____

142. What are the things you have done in your life that you would say you are proudest of?

_____

_____

_____

_____

_____

_____

_____

_____

_____

_____

143. I would like to get an idea of what a day in your life is like. Can you tell me what you did yesterday? Begin with when you woke up and go through the day as you experienced it.

_____

_____

_____

_____

_____

_____

_____

_____

_____

_____

_____

_____

_____

_____

_____

_____

_____

_____

_____

_____

144. What suggestions do you have for givers of mental health care for making mental health care more useful to you?

_____

_____
_____
_____
_____
_____
_____
_____
_____
_____
_____

Thank you for answering all these questions for me. (Pay person.) One of the special things about the study is that we would like to understand how people change over time. I would like to interview you again in six months to find out what things have happened in your life. You will be paid $10 again. Is there a phone number where you can be reached? _____

Thanks very much for your time. I will contact you again.

Ending time _____

INTERVIEWER: Is there material in this interview that would make good quotes?

YES..1
NO 2

Question #	Page #
_____	_____
_____	_____
_____	_____
_____	_____
_____	_____
_____	_____
_____	_____

Interviewer's Ratings and Comments

1. Generally, how well did S seem to understand the questions?

VERY WELL 4
SOMEWHAT..3
NEEDED MUCH PROBING.....................2
NOT AT ALL..1

2. Generally, how well was S able to focus on questions?

VERY WELL 3
SOMEWHAT 2
NOT AT ALL..1

3. Generally, the content of the responses was:

	A GREAT DEAL	SOME-WHAT	NOT AT ALL
Logical	2	1	0
Coherent	2	1	0
Relevant	2	1	0
Rambling	0	1	2

4. During the interview S was:

	TO A LARGE EXTENT	TO SOME EXTENT	NOT AT ALL
Friendly	2	1	0
Cooperative	2	1	0
Hostile	0	1	2
Able to maintain eye contact with interviewer	2	1	0
Able to respond freely to most questions	2	1	0
Willing to answer many questions	2	1	0
Fabricating	0	1	2

5. Generally did S seem . . .

	A GREAT DEAL	SOME-WHAT	NOT AT ALL
Alert?	2	1	0
Confused?	0	1	2
Withdrawn?	0	1	2
Lethargic?	0	1	2
Depressed?	0	1	2
Agitated?	0	1	2
Preoccupied?	0	1	2
Denying?	0	1	2
Devoid of emotion (flat affect)?	0	1	2
Sleepy?	0	1	2
Other? (specify)	0	1	2

---

6. Did S engage in the following behaviors?

	A GREAT DEAL	SOME-WHAT	NOT AT ALL
Pacing	0	1	2
Nervous smoking	0	1	2

Rocking	0	1	2
Fidgeting	0	1	2
Gesturing	0	1	2
Inappropriate laughing and giggling	0	1	2
Keeping rigid posture	0	1	2
Keeping slumped posture	0	1	2

7. Rate S's grooming and hygiene along the following continuum.

Neat/clean	5	4	3	2	1	Untidy/dirty
Generally appropriate	5	4	3	2	1	Generally inappropriate/bizarre

8. Overall did S act appropriately?

ALL THE TIME 4
MOST OF THE TIME 3
SOME OF THE TIME 2
NOT AT ALL 1

9. How did S generally seem affected by the interview?

	MOST OF THE TIME	SOME OF THE TIME	NOT AT ALL
Interested	2	1	0
Bored	0	1	2
Upset	0	1	2
Comfortable	2	1	0
Pleased to be interviewed	2	1	0
Annoyed at being interviewed	0	1	2

Please add comment or concerns about S or how the interview went:

NAMES, ADDRESSES AND PHONE NUMBERS OF PERSONS WHO KNOW WHEREABOUTS OF S.
COPY OFF CONSENT FORM.

NAME _____ RELATIONSHIP _____

ADDRESS _____

PHONE _____

NAME _____ RELATIONSHIP _____

ADDRESS _____

PHONE _____

SELECT BIBLIOGRAPHY

Aldenderfer, M., & Blashfield, R. (1984). *Cluster analysis*. Beverly Hills, CA: Sage.

American Psychiatric Association. (1980). *Diagnostic and statistical manual of mental disorders* (3rd ed.). Washington, DC: Author.

Anthony, W. A., Buell, G. J., Sharratt, S., & Althoff, M. E. (1972). Efficacy of psychiatric rehabilitation. *Psychological Bulletin, 78*(6), 447–456.

Arnhoff, F. N. (1975). Social consequences of policy toward mental illness. *Science, 188,* 1277–1281.

Ashley, M. (1922). Outcome of 1,000 cases paroled from the Middletown State Homeopathic Hospital. *State Hospital Quarterly, 8,* 64–70.

Bachrach, L. (1986). Deinstitutionalization: What do the numbers mean? *Hospital and Community Psychiatry, 37,* 118–121.

Bassuk, E. L., & Gerson, S. (1978). Deinstitutionalization and mental health services. *Scientific American, 238*(2), 46–53.

Blumenthal, R. D., Kreisman, D., & O'Connor, P. (1982). Return to the family and its consequence for rehospitalization among recently discharged mental patients. *Psychological Medicine, 12,* 141–147.

Brennan, T. (1987). Classification: An overview of selected methodological issues. In D. M. Gottfredson & M. Tonry (Eds.), *Prediction and classification: Criminal justice decision making* (pp. 201–248). Chicago: University of Chicago Press.

Brill, H., & Malzberg, B. (1962). *Statistical report on the arrest record of male ex-patients, age 16 and over, released from New York state mental hospitals during the period 1946–48* (Mental Hospital Services Supplemental Report 135). Washington, DC: American Psychiatric Association.

Cocozza, J. J., Melick, M. E., & Steadman, H. J. (1978). Trends in violent crime among ex-mental patients. *Criminology, 16,* 317–334.

Cohen, L., & Freeman, H. (1945). How dangerous to the community are state mental patients? *Connecticut State Medical Journal, 9,* 697–700.

Cohen, S. (1985). *Visions of social control*. Cambridge, MA: Polity Press.

Cook, F. L., Jencks, C., Mayer, S., Constantino, E., & Popkin, S. (1986). *Stability and change in economic hardship: Chicago 1983–1985.* Evanston, IL: Northwestern University, Center for Urban Affairs and Policy Research.

Donnelly, J. (1978). Confidentiality: The myth and the reality. In W. E. Barton & C. J. Sanborn (Eds.), *Law and the mental health professions: Friction at the interface* (pp. 185–205). New York: International Universities Press.

Durbin, J. R., Pasewark, R. A., & Albers, D. (1977). Criminality and mental illness: A study of arrest rates in a rural state. *American Journal of Psychiatry, 134,* 80–83.

Endicott, J., & Spitzer, R. L. (1978). A diagnostic interview: The schedule for affective disorders and schizophrenia. *Archives of General Psychiatry, 35,* 837–844.

Endicott, J., Spitzer, R. L., Fleiss, J. L., & Cohen, J. (1976). The global assessment scale: A procedure for measuring overall severity of psychiatric disturbance. *Archives of General Psychiatry, 33,* 766–771.

Ennis, B. J. (1972). *Prisoners of psychiatry: Mental patients, psychiatrists and the law.* New York: Harcourt Brace Jovanovich.

Franklin, J. L., Kittredge, L. D., & Thrasher, J. H. (1975). A survey of factors related to mental hospital readmissions. *Hospital and Community Psychiatry, 26*(11), 749–751.

Giovannoni, J., & Gurel, L. (1967). Socially disruptive behavior of ex-mental patients. *Archives of General Psychiatry, 17*(2), 146–153.

Goffman, E. (1961). *Asylums.* Chicago: Aldine Press.

Goldstrom, I. D., & Manderscheid, R. W. (1982). The chronically mentally ill: A descriptive analysis from the uniform client data instrument. *Community Support Service Journal, 2*(3), 4–9.

Gottfredson, D. M., & Tonry, M. (Eds.) (1987). *Prediction and classification: Criminal justice decision making.* Chicago: University of Chicago Press.

Greenblatt, M., Sharaf, M. R., & Stone, E. M. (1971). *The dynamics of institutional change.* Pittsburgh: University of Pittsburgh Press.

Greenblatt, M., York, R., & Brown, E. L. (1955). *From custodial to therapeutic patient care in mental hospitals.* New York: Russell Sage Foundation.

Greenley, J. R. (1979). Family symptom tolerance and rehospitalization experience of psychiatric patients. *Research in Community and Mental Health, 1,* 357–386.

Gruenberg, E. M., & Archer, J. (1979). Abandonment of responsibility for the seriously mentally ill. *Health and Society, 57*(4), 485–506.

Gusfield, J. (1975, Fall). Categories of ownership and responsibility in social issues: Alcohol abuse and automobile use. *Journal of Drug Addiction, 5,* 285–303.

Hartigan, J. A. (1975). *Clustering algorithms.* New York: John Wiley & Sons.

Havens, L. (1987). *Approaches to the mind: Movement of the psychiatric schools from sects toward science*. Cambridge, MA: Harvard University Press.

Jacobs, J. B. (1977). *Stateville: The penitentiary in mass society*. Chicago: University of Chicago Press.

Joint Commission on Mental Illness and Health. (1961). *Action for mental health*. New York: Basic Books.

Kleinman, A. (1980). *Patient and healers in the context of culture*. Berkeley, CA: University of California Press.

Lagos, J., Perlmutter, K., & Saexinger, H. (1977). Fear of the mentally ill: Empirical support for the common man. *American Journal of Psychiatry, 134*, 1134–1137.

Lehman, A. F., Ward, N. C., & Linn, L. S. (1982). Chronic mental patients: The quality of life issue. *American Journal of Psychiatry, 139*(10), 1271–1276.

Lerman, P. (1982). *Deinstitutionalization and the welfare state*. New Brunswick, NJ: Rutgers University Press.

Lewis, D. A., & Hugi, R. (1981). Therapeutic stations and the chronically treated mentally ill. *Social Service Review, 55*(2), 206–220.

Lewis, D. A., Pavkov, T., Rosenberg, H., Reed, S., Lurigio, A., Kalifon, Z., Johnson, B., & Riger, S. (1987). *State hospital utilization in Chicago: People, problems and policy*. Evanston, IL: Northwestern University, Center for Urban Affairs and Policy Research.

Lipton, F. R., Sabatini, A., & Katz, S. (1983). Down and out in the city: The homeless mentally ill. *Hospital and Community Psychiatry, 34*(9), 817–821.

Lurigio, A. J. (1986). *Measuring recidivism in probation*. Chicago: Cook County Adult Probation Department.

Lurigio, A. J., & Lewis, D. A. (1987). The criminal mental patient: A descriptive analysis and suggestions for future research. *Criminal Justice and Behavior, 14*(3), 268–287.

Minkoff, K. (1978). A map of chronic mental patients. In J. A. Talbott (Ed.), *The chronic mental patient* (pp. 11–32). Washington, DC: American Psychiatric Association.

Monahan, J., & Steadman, H. J. (1983). Crime and mental disorder: An epidemiological approach. In M. Tonry & N. Morris (Eds.), *Crime and justice: An annual review of research* (pp. 145–189). Chicago: University of Chicago Press.

Monahan, J., & Steadman, H. J. (1984). *Crime and mental disorder*, Washington, DC: U.S. Department of Justice, National Institute of Justice.

Morrissey, J. P. (1982). Deinstitutionalizing the mentally ill: Process, outcomes, and new directions. In W. R. Gove (Ed.), *Deviance and mental illness* (pp. 147–176). Newbury Park, CA: Sage.

Perrucci, R. (1974). *Circle of madness: On being insane and institutionalized in America*. Englewood Cliffs, NJ: Prentice-Hall.

Pollock, H. (1938). Is the paroled patient a menace to the community? *Psychiatric Quarterly, 12,* 236–244.

Rabkin, J. (1979). Criminal behavior of discharged mental patients: A critical appraisal of the research. *Psychological Bulletin, 86,* 1–27.

Ragan, J. F., Jr. (1974). *Mental health and developmental disabilities in Illinois: An examination*. Springfield, IL: Illinois Department of Mental Health and Developmental Disabilities.

Rainwater, L. (1974). *What money buys: Inequality and the social meanings of income*. New York: Basic Books.

Rappeport, J. R., & Lassen, G. (1965). Dangerousness–arrest rate comparisons of discharged patients and the general population. *American Journal of Psychiatry, 121,* 776–783.

Redlich, F., & Kellert, S. R. (1978). Trends in American mental health. *American Journal of Psychiatry, 135*(1), 22–28.

Reich, R. (1973). Care of the chronically mentally ill: A national disgrace. *American Journal of Psychiatry, 130*(8), 911–912.

Roesch, R., & Golding, S. L. (1985). The impact of deinstitutionalization. In D. P. Farrington & J. Gunn (Eds.), *Aggression and dangerous* (pp. 209–239). John Wiley & Sons.

Rosenblatt, A., & Mayer, J. (1974). The recidivism of mental patients: A review of past studies. *American Journal of Orthopsychiatry, 44*(5), 697–708.

Rothman, D. (1980). *Conscience and convenience*. Boston: Little, Brown.

Schmidt, L. J., Reinhard, A. M., Kane, R. L., & Olsen, D. M. (1977). The mentally ill in nursing homes. *Archives of General Psychiatry, 34,* 687–691.

Scull, A. T. (1977). *Decarceration: Community treatment and the deviant: A radical view*. Englewood Cliffs, NJ: Prentice-Hall.

Segal, S. P., & Aviram, U. (1979). Reintegrating the mentally ill in the community. *International Journal of Rehabilitation Research, 2*(4), 499–506.

Shadish, W. R., Straw, R. B., McSweeney, A. J., Koller, D. L., & Bootzin, R. R. (1981). Nursing home care for mental patients: Descriptive data and some propositions. *American Journal of Community Psychology, 9*(5), 617–633.

Solomon, P. L., Gordon, B. H., & Davis, J. M. (1984). *Community services to discharged patients*. Springfield, IL: Charles C. Thomas.

Sosowsky, L. (1980). Explaining the increased arrest rate among mental patients: A cautionary note. *American Journal of Psychiatry, 137,* 1602–1605.

Stone, A. A. (1982). Psychiatric abuse and legal reform: Two ways to make a bad situation worse. *International Journal of Law and Psychiatry, 5,* 9–28.

Talbott, J. A. (Ed.) (1984). *The chronic mental patient: Recent research and developments.* Orlando, FL: Grune & Stratton.

Taylor, D. G. (1986). *Public opinion and collective action: The Boston school desegregation conflict.* Chicago: University of Chicago Press.

Teplin, L. A. (1984). Criminalizing mental disorder: The comparative arrest rate of the mentally ill. *American Psychologist, 39,* 794–803.

Teplin, L. A. (1985). The criminality of the mentally ill: A dangerous misconception. *American Journal of Psychiatry, 142,* 593–599.

Treffert, D. A. (1974). Dying with their rights on. *Prism, 2,* 49–52.

Warren, C. A. B. (1981). New forms of social control: The myth of deinstitutionalization. *American Behavioral Scientist, 24*(6), 724–740.

Zitrin, A., Hardesty, A. S., & Burdock, E. L. (1976). Crime and violence among mental patients. *American Journal of Psychiatry, 133,* 142–146.

INDEX

DAN A. LEWIS, Ph.D., is Associated Director of the Center for Urban Affairs and Policy Research at Northwestern University and Chairman of the Graduate Program in Human Development and Social Policy at the School of Education and Social Policy at Northwestern University. His research interests include the sociological analysis of urban problems (crime, mental illness, education, etc.) with special emphasis on the importance of social and political theory in policy development.

STEPHANIE RIGER is a Professor of Psychology at Lake Forest College and a Research Associate at the Center for Urban Affairs, Northwestern University. Her latest book, *The Female Fear,* was published last year by Free Press.

HELEN ROSENBERG recently completed her doctorate in sociology at Northwestern University and is currently doing research at Thresholds, Inc., in Chicago.

HENDRIK WAGENAAR received his doctorate from the Massachusetts Institute of Technology. He is currently a Research Associate at the Massachusetts Mental Health Center in Boston.

ARTHUR J. LURIGIO is an Assistant Professor of Criminal Justice and Psychology at Loyola University in Chicago.

SUSAN REED recently completed her doctorate in Human Development and Social Policy in the School of Education and Social Policy at Northwestern University. She is currently a Research Associate at the Center for Urban Affairs at Northwestern.